Archaeology and International
Development in Africa

DUCKWORTH DEBATES IN ARCHAEOLOGY

Series editor: Richard Hodges

Archaeology and International Development in Africa

Colin Breen
&
Daniel Rhodes

Duckworth

First published in 2010 by
Gerald Duckworth & Co. Ltd.
90-93 Cowcross Street, London EC1M 6BF
Tel: 020 7490 7300
Fax: 020 7490 0080
info@duckworth-publishers.co.uk
www.ducknet.co.uk

A catalogue record for this book is available
from the British Library

ISBN 978-0-7156-3905-4

Typeset by Ray Davies

Contents

Contents

List of Illustrations

Figures

List of Illustrations

Tables

Abbreviations

ADB	African Development Bank
AKTC	Aga Khan Trust for Culture
AU	African Union
CHDA	Centre for Heritage Development in Africa
CraTerre-EAG	Centre International de la Construction en Terre
CHM	Cultural Heritage Management
CRM	Cultural Resource Management
DfID	Department for International Development (UK)
EIA	Environmental Impact Assessment
EPA	Environmental Protection Agency
EU	European Union
EC	European Commission
GDP	Gross Domestic Product
HER	Historic Environment Record
IBRD	International Bank for Reconstruction and Development
ICCROM	International Centre for the Study of the Preservation and Restoration of Cultural Property
ICOMOS	International Council on Monuments and Sites
ITFCSD	Italian Trust Fund for Culture and Sustainable Development
IMF	International Monetary Fund
MDGs	Millennium Development Goals
MENA	Middle East and North Africa
NCAM	National Corporation of Antiquities and Museums
NGO	Non-Governmental Organization
NMK	National Museums of Kenya
ODA	Overseas Development Administration/ Aid
SAA	Society for American Archaeology
SAfA	Society of Africanist Archaeologists
SAREC	Swedish Agency for Research Cooperation with Developing Countries

Abbreviations

SIDA	Swedish International Development Authority
SMR	Sites and Monuments Record
UN	United Nations
UNDP	United Nations Development Programme
UNED	United Nations Environment Programme
UNESCO	United Nations Educational, Scientific and Cultural Organization
UNICEF	United Nations Children's Fund
USAID	United States Agency for International Development
WAC	World Archaeology Congress

Preface and Acknowledgements

This book arose out of a number of years of questioning and doubt. It is likely that many people at some stage in their careers begin to question the validity of what they are doing and the direction their career has taken them. Is what they do valuable or beneficial? Is there any validity in their career choice? Are they actually making any difference to society and would they be better investing their energies in a different direction or in a different place? These questions have all haunted us over the past number of years working as academic archaeologists in a Western university environment. They became especially pronounced after a decade of working in various countries throughout sub-Saharan Africa when directly confronted by the seemingly mountainous problems that these countries faced. Issues of poverty, hunger, war and environment change loomed large as we engaged in the luxury of practising what many would perceive to be an elitist and, albeit interesting, hobbyist profession. There remained a constant feeling that maybe we could be doing something better, devoting our energies and resources to more pressing needs and issues across the continent. There were justifications, of course. Ultimately we were doing no harm and the same could not be said for the myriad of vested economic and political interests across the region. We were not trading arms, we were not exploiting a country's resources, we were not engaged in corruption, etc. But there had to be more. Of course the traditional, almost antiquarian, practice of Western archaeology in Africa had to change. It was not, or at least should not be, acceptable to come in as an individual engaging in careerist

11

research before withdrawing to a remote ivory tower to write and theorize. Most Africanist archaeologists now recognize that they have greater responsibilities in terms of dissemination, resource protection and the delivery of training opportunities. But there can be still more. Archaeology has the potential to integrate into the broader framework of international development in Africa and contribute towards bringing about 'good change'. This book is an attempt to map out some preliminary thoughts on how such integration can be realized. It should not be read as a definitive study but is rather presented as an initial argument and a basis for future discussion.

The ultimate prompt for this book came when one of the authors had the good fortune to share a taxi in Khartoum with an Irish aid worker engaged by a major Irish aid organization. Our team had just returned from three weeks' excavation at the historic port town of Suakin on Sudan's Red Sea coast. She had just returned from months of activity in Darfur at the outset of the recent conflict and genocide. I was profoundly embarrassed! What we were doing was worthless in comparison to the work being undertaken by her organization. With more mature reflection the conservation and investigation of a nation's heritage, coupled with dedicated efforts at building heritage capacity, was of course not worthless, but still seemed isolated and removed from the work of the development agencies. There simply had to be a more engaged and informed way of carrying out our work. What follows is an exploration of potential avenues of integration and co-operation rooted in dialogue.

Many people are owed thanks for stimulating our interest in this area and for constant help for two authors who are still very much novices, dipping into the rich arena of African archaeological studies. They include: Wes Forsythe for his professionalism and companionship on all of our journeys, Paul Lane for starting much of this, Michael Mallinson for always pushing, John Mack for innovation and inspiration, Mark Horton for academic engagement, Gabriel Cooney for belief, Brian Williams for energy, Rory Quinn, Thomas McErlean and Rosemary McConkey for unrivalled collegiality, J.D. Hill for future developments, Laurence Smith for all he does, Lucy Blue for similarities, Felix Chami for African brilliance, Dave Eastwood and Andrew Cooper for enabling it all to start, Gerry Breen for family and professional presence, Donal Boland for all of the above. Other companions have included Athman Lali Omar, Eddie McPhilips, Bernie Lafferty, John Joe McGettigan, John O'Raw, Cian Boland, Jacke Philips, Chris McGonigle, Eoghan Kieran, Ted Pollard, Stephanie Wynne-Jones, Mjema Elinaza and Joseph Matua. Thanks (again) to Killian McDaid for finalizing the diagrams at short notice.

Special thanks go to Deborah Blake at Duckworth for bringing this to fruition and for all her work on the volume.

For

Claire (CB)
Yvonne and Peter Wilson (DR)

1

Introduction

This short volume is about the creation of opportunity and capacity. It is a book about overcoming adversities and negativity and the use of archaeology and heritage to aid the empowerment of community in Africa. Recent popular African history has been witness to decades of conflict, famine, poverty and environmental disaster. Both the print and broadcast media portray a continent on its knees beset by seemingly insurmountable problems on a daily basis. Many people suffer from Africa fatigue, in which the sheer scale of the problems and continual bombardment of terrible imagery has led them simply to turn away from the place. The numbers are staggering and verging on the unfathomable. The millions of people killed in the Congo over the last few decades scarcely warrant a sentence or two in our newspapers, which are instead obsessed by the often extravagant lives of a string of ever-changing celebrities. It often seems that the cult of celebrity has emerged as the dominant paradigm in contemporary society over issues such as social justice or environment change.

But Africa is too complex a continent to be merely labelled a failed place. It is not all bad news. There are many sides to its societies; stable and unstable, prosperous and less prosperous, rich and poor, corrupt and courageous. Similarly, while Africa's environment can sometimes be volatile and dangerous, it is also one of its strongest assets. Its diversity, scale and sheer beauty have in turn been the focus of past civilizations and contemporary society. The many physical remnants of these societies are impressive reminders of a dynamic past. Contrary to what many early European travellers said, Africa was not a dark continent with only a primitive and tribal past; instead it was the cradle of humanity that subsequently saw the cyclical development of societies and groupings. From the kingdom states of Egypt in the North, the medieval Swahili towns on the East coast, the historic settlements along the South African littoral, to the historic kingships of West Africa, the continent has seen intense cultural activity over many millennia. Similarly, Africa's landscapes and environment have been subject to continual change, epitomized by the radical changes in the Sahara, previously a lush savannah in places (Fig. 1).

Contemporary African society and landscape is likewise subject to continual change and upheaval. Unfortunately, owing to a series of historical and modern interventions, colonial activity, poor governance and corruption, environment change and economic exclusionary policies, many countries and communities across the continent remain heavily marginalized with fairly endemic problems across societal frameworks. The past few decades have seen the emergence of an international development framework designed to alleviate Africa's problems and bring about change. The relative merits and successes of this remain contested, but aid and development work constitutes a central pivot of the agendas of the international community as evidenced through the programmes of the United Nations, the World Bank and most Global North countries. Much of this work has been economically focussed, with health, education and gender issues gaining priority. Environment has increasingly become a dominant focus with issues of climate and environment change coming to the forefront of policy priority. Resource availability and management remain key issues. Natural resources such as minerals, forest, water and soils spring readily to mind when we conceptualize these issues, but heritage, and in particular the tangible built heritage, must also be regarded as a resource and one that can integrate and contribute to international development work.

It can be strongly argued that archaeological sites, landscapes and material culture are perceived as having an economic value and a public benefit. Archaeology can also be

Fig. 1. Map of Africa.

viewed as a resource, one that is inclusive and not merely delineated by environmental parameters. Built heritage enhances landscape, encourages memory and is an integral part of social fabric. To begin to assign value to such a resource is contentious but it undoubtedly has a symbolic value and can be used to develop understandings of past and current constructions of national and social identities and ease social integration. The archaeological resource contains key data on past landscape and environmental change and societal shifts throughout the region. There are also tangible economic benefits measurable though the heritage industry and tourism. Community involvement with heritage can lead to empowerment, employment and educational enhancement, all integral components of contemporary development activity. However,

the linkages between archaeology and international development are rarely made. There are many reasons for this
associated with traditional academic practice, the insularity of
the subject area and an unwillingness to engage in discourse in
terms of subject value and direction. An alternative perspective
is offered here to stimulate debate and, we hope, action. It
should be stressed that this study does not aspire to be exhaustive; it is offered as a discursive overview presenting a brief
examination of current practice.

Aims

This volume has then a number of general aims:

1. To highlight the practice, issues, threats and problems
associated with the research, management and protection of
the archaeological resource in Africa.
2. To examine the linkages between archaeology and contemporary international development practice.
3. To suggest ways in which both archaeologists and the
archaeological resource can contribute to sustainable environmental and economic practices and contribute in proactive and
beneficial ways to African society.

Africa's archaeological resource

There is a tendency from a Northern perspective to regard
Africa almost as an immense island or a cohesive cultural unit.
However, it is a huge continent with diverse countries made up
of many peoples, landscapes and ecologies. Africa's histories
are as complex as they are long. The earliest global evidence for
our first ancestors comes from the Rift Valley regions of the
north-eastern part of the continent. While it is likely that we
can trace our evolutionary lineage back eight million years to
this region, it is with the development of tool technology about
three million years ago, known as the general Olduwan tradition of stone-knapping or flaking, that we can begin to identify

tangible material culture. *Homo erectus* were users of this technology around 1.8 million years ago and also used fire for warmth, cooking and social purposes (Barham 2008: 102). Greater complexity in this technology emerges during the Acheulean phase about 1.6 million years ago. The earliest existing evidence for woodworking comes from 1.5 million years ago while the earliest wooden tools date to 200,000 years ago from the Kalambo Falls site (Gowlett 2008: 101). The use of wooden shafts or handles marks a fundamental shift in technological progression and signals the transition into the Middle Stone Age. This technology was used by *Homo heidelbergensis* with brains comparable in size to those of modern humans (Barham 2008: 103). Early Middle Stone Age artefacts were found on an emerged reef terrace on the Red Sea coast of Eritrea, dated to the last interglacial (about 125,000 years ago) while similar discoveries have been made in cave sites such as Blombos in South Africa. These finds demonstrate that early humans occupied coastal areas and exploited near-shore marine food resources by this time, the earliest well-dated evidence for human adaptation to a coastal marine environment. Around two million years ago populations began to leave Africa and spread out into Europe and Asia, and later migrations included the movement of early humans north and eastwards up to 40,000 years ago. This later Palaeolithic phase is still generally referred to as the Stone Age, technological change emerging only in the first millennium AD with the development of iron technology. Many parts of sub-Saharan Africa are viewed as having bypassed the Neolithic and Bronze Ages, although a number of scholars have countered this with recent findings from Cameroon and Zanzibar (Chami 2006).

The use of iron becomes apparent from the sixth century BC onwards, although its adoption is variable. Throughout the last few millennia, Africa has functioned within a number of marine systems and has been subject to a wide variety of both internal and external cultural influences. Along North Africa's coast cultural activity was dominated by trade and conquest throughout the Mediterranean region. The great kingdoms of

Egypt emerged about 5,000 years ago, following significant climate change that brought a series of groups together along the Nile (Hornung 1999). Later Greek, Roman and subsequent Byzantine activity was also centred here with the Nile and its delta playing a pivotal role in the development of society and economy across this region. Tangible remains of these periods include the pyramid tombs of the pharaohs and the classical towns of the Romans. Extraordinary finds, including inscribed columns, shipwrecks and foundations have been made underwater at the Egyptian port of Alexandria, where the Pharos lighthouse was built during the Ptolemaic period. The town was named after Alexander the Great and subsequently became one of the major trading centres of the classical world and a centre for intellectual pursuit, epitomized by its library. Other significant ports included the Phoenician foundations at Carthage in Tunisia and Tripoli in Libya.

The Red Sea region was closely related to the Mediterranean system, initially with overland caravan routes north through the desert and up the Nile (the continuity of which was maintained in the more recent past with the construction of the Suez Canal). This was an important trading and migrant system throughout the historical period, as exemplified by the Roman period ports at Berenike and Quseir al-Qadim in Egypt and later medieval ports such as Suakin in the Sudan and Adulis in Eritrea. The Ascara Island shipwreck, Eritrea, dated on the basis of ceramic finds to around the seventh century AD, testifies to the continued importance of coastal movement in this region, while the eighteenth-century shipwreck at Sadana Island, Egypt, is evidence of the globalized nature of trade with its cargo of coffee, spices and Chinese export porcelain. A series of interior kingdoms played an integral part in this system. The Aksumite Empire, for example, centred on the town of Aksum and the port of Adulis, controlled much of the Ethiopian and Eritrean highlands for the greater part of the first millennium. Later the Ottoman Empire came to dominate much of the Red Sea region.

1. Introduction

Fig. 2. Fort Jesus, Mombasa, Kenya in the 1840s (J.L. Karpf, *Travels, Researches and Missionary Labour* London, 1968, 2nd edn).

The Indian Ocean system in turn is dominated by the monsoon that controls much of its sea-based traffic. There has been a long tradition of coastal archaeology undertaken along the East African coast, examining medieval 'Swahili' settlement, towns with architecturally significant stone-built buildings which were engaged in extensive hinterland and foreland trade between the African interior and the broader Indian Ocean. Further inland significant centres of power and prestige built up and were centred on places like Great Zimbabwe. Subsequent European and Arab colonial expansion is visible archaeologically along this coast. Fort Jesus at Mombasa is a significant physical expression of fortification and control of mercantile seaways (Fig. 2). The wreck of the *Santo Antonio de Tanna*, sunk in 1696-7 during the course of an Omani siege of Fort Jesus, represents the well-preserved remains of a Portuguese frigate lying on the seabed beneath the walls of the fort. Similar colonial period architecture dominates sections of the South African coastline where a number of important state-sponsored coastal surveys and management programmes have been initiated. Important waterfront excavations have taken place in Cape Town and on shipwrecks

21

such as the Dutch East Indiaman *Oosterland,* lost in Table Bay in 1697.

While research has been relatively limited across the West African region, it has been possible to identify early horizons associated with the use of iron. A number of sites in Nigeria have been examined while later usage has been identified in Sierra Leone and the Liberian hinterland from the eighth century onwards (DeCorse 2001: 4). Extensive trade networks across the Sahel developed throughout the first millennium and a number of major polities emerged, including ancient Ghana, Asanti and Benin (Insoll 1996). A number of urban sites in Mali play a central role in this trade. In particular the later centuries of the second millennium see continual change across the west with the rise and fall of states, the expansion of Islam and environment change (DeCorse 2001: 1). West Africa also becomes part of a wider globalized network from the sixteenth century onwards, when European mercantile and slaving activity works with a number of regional power bases to systematically exploit both natural and human resources. This coastline has experienced limited archaeological research, yet future investigations should ultimately add significantly to our understandings of pre-European contact activity, early exploration and historical analysis of the emergent Atlantic slave system within the broader Atlantic social world. Recent investigations have taken place at the former port of Elimna, Ghana, the first European slave-trading post in sub-Saharan Africa, built in 1482. However, as in other parts of Africa, a number of commercially led underwater operations have been undertaken along the west coast and at offshore islands such as Cape Verde. This type of operation poses a significant risk to the future protection and management of the marine archaeological resource and establishes a negative precedent for other African countries. International attention and recent initiatives led by UNESCO should go some way to discourage these operations in future.

In terms of industrial heritage, the structural and material remains associated with the extractive industries remain much understudied (Worth 2008: 107). Yet there are extensive remains associated with gold and diamond mining in South Africa, salt extraction across much of the Sahel, glass works at the Cape, and tin and copper in Nigeria, Zambia and the DRC. Colonial era plantation sites still survive across the continent, including clove and coconut farms along the East African littoral, bean production in many parts of the north-east and forestry in the central regions. Transport and communications are a key factor in facilitating the development of industry, and significant work remains to be done on the development of infrastructure and travel networks across the continent. The railways in particular parallel colonial advance and enterprise and represent a physical means with which to subjugate a continent.

There is also recognition of the close relationship between archaeology and ethnographic practice. In particular, heritage often has a symbolic rather than an aesthetic value across many parts of Africa. Societies often lay emphasis on special places and traditions such as ritual and music rather than sites and architecture (UNESCO 2003: 40). Many natural places without monumentality play a central cultural role for certain communities. This difference still poses problems for many Western heritage practitioners who try to assign Northern value and practice to cultural heritage management across Africa.

Issues and threats

We recognize the wealth of archaeological remains, material culture and built heritage across Africa. What is also important to realize in this context is the myriad issues associated with the sustainability of this cultural resource. A wide variety of threats, both natural and cultural, impact upon the resource, while the socio-economic and political circumstances of the continent directly effect resource development. Specifically, the level of political instability and poverty places landscapes, sites and artefacts under severe pressure. Of course we must also recognize the reasons why the protection of archaeological material has been given low priority in many countries faced with major problems of war and famine. It is not argued here that archaeology should become the pre-eminent concern among development workers, and no blame is apportioned here in that direction. Rather, we must first assess and quantify both the resource and the level of risk associated with it and then begin to develop strategies for its management and, dare we say it at this early stage, its sustainable development and exploitation. A brief overview of the level of threat is presented here with a rapid introduction to the broader context of management and protection. These issues will be expanded upon in Chapter 3.

It is probably not possible to assign a hierarchy of threat at present. There is neither sufficient data relating to the extent of landscape change nor adequate information on the resource as a whole to allow this. Instead we can probably group resource threats under three primary headings: natural and environmental impacts, human impact and institutional neglect (Fig. 3).

Environment change is not a recent phenomenon in Africa. The continent has seen continual fluctuations in temperature and climatic conditions over many millennia, giving rise to continual changes in landscape cover and ecological conditions. What is relevant here is the pace of environment change over the last four decades. The rapid and quantifiable pace of desertification across much of Northern Africa has lead to encroachment upon sites of particular importance. The increased rate of coastal erosion along the East African coast has lead to the loss of significant cultural remains. This erosion is often associated with the depletion of mangrove cover for development purposes. Elsewhere increased rainfall and flooding events have severely impacted upon monuments. Such impacts cannot be ascribed simply to natural processes of change; instead they are linked to the massive increase in human activity across the continent over the past 100 years. Consequent human

Issues/Processes   **Impacts**

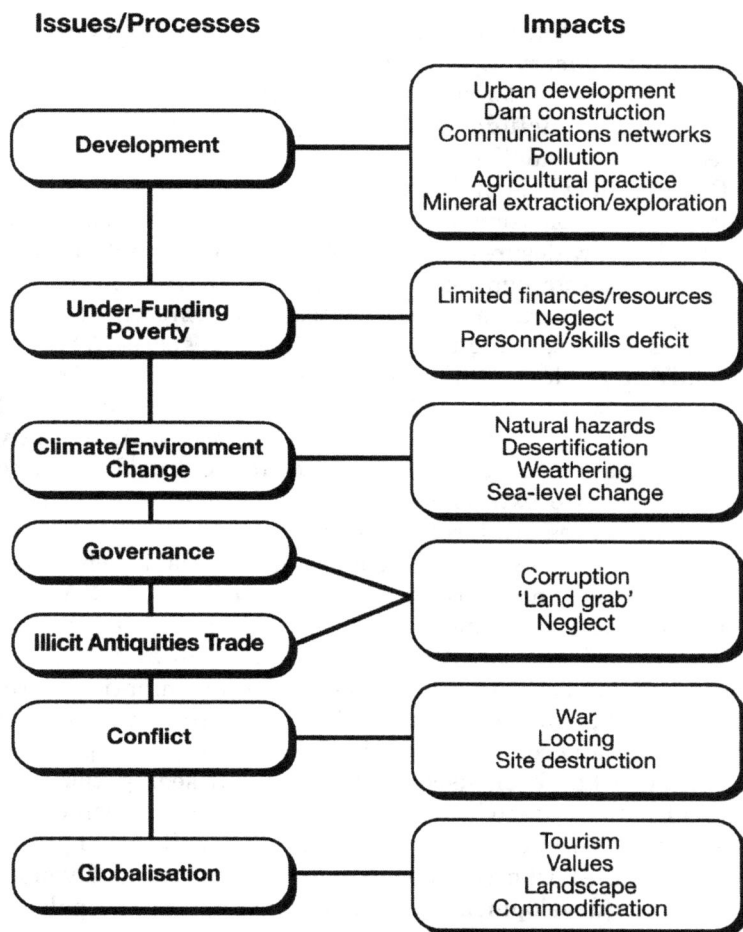

Development	Urban development Dam construction Communications networks Pollution Agricultural practice Mineral extraction/exploration
Under-Funding Poverty	Limited finances/resources Neglect Personnel/skills deficit
Climate/Environment Change	Natural hazards Desertification Weathering Sea-level change
Governance Illicit Antiquities Trade	Corruption 'Land grab' Neglect
Conflict	War Looting Site destruction
Globalisation	Tourism Values Landscape Commodification

Fig. 3. Issues and threats facing the archaeological
resource in Africa.

impacts on the resource include the expansion of unsympathetic urban development that encroaches upon earlier areas of
important built remains. Commercial development, whether it
is for infrastructural purposes, tourism or business, poses a
major risk to the structural integrity of sites, but we must

recognize the need to balance the necessity for such development with conservation concerns. The commodification of landscape for tourist reasons is a growing concern. Other human impacts include illicit antiquities trade, souvenir collection and vandalism.

Finally, the whole problem of poor governance coupled with a shortage of professional capacity remains a major issue. This has lead to a widespread neglect of the resource and an overdependence on foreign researchers for conservation funds and investigative programmes. Few states have comprehensive inventories of sites, while museum provision is sparse. There is virtually no implementation of Environmental Impact Assessment even where required by law, and conservation and heritage management expertise remain weak. University courses in archaeology, conservation and cultural resource management are extremely limited. A number of externally funded initiatives to address these shortcomings are underway but their perceived success levels has been variable. The overt willingness of Global North academics to facilitate this process has often exacerbated the problem and can lead to the theoretical concern of who is setting the conservation and research agenda in many of the countries under examination here. Aligned to this has been the politicized nature of archaeology practice in many countries both in the past and recent present. Archaeology has been used to justify racial segregation and cultural superiority (Garlake 1982). It has been adopted by nationalist movements and was associated with attempts to create a pan-African commonality, overriding tribal division, through the development of common ancestry at the paleontological sites in Kenya and Tanzania (Schmidt 1995). The incorporation of the castle and fort sites on the west coast into a diasporan heritage tourism framework and the emergent UNESCO 'slave route' initiative are also pertinent, given the complex historical structure of slaving and the highly contested nature of its interpretation and understanding (Stahl 2009) (Fig. 4).

1. Introduction

Fig. 4. Slave memorial, Zanzibar Stone Town.

Previous related work

While a number of related subject areas have made concerted attempts to integrate within the international development framework, archaeology has been more reticent. Anthropology in particular has long been aware of its position in development studies, albeit from differing and often contentious perspectives. 'Applied anthropology' has worked within the social spheres of agriculture and industry, while there is also a history of anthropologists working with colonial administrators in Africa. The extent to which they actually supported these regimes is debatable. Some probably actively resisted, with many simply being ignored (Gardner & Lewis 1996). Archaeologists, of course, also worked within the colonial governments but mostly practised their subject as a hobby with it rarely featuring as part of colonial policy. It then manifested itself as a Westernist subject founded in Northern narratives.

In 1990, Peter Schmidt, then president of the Society of Africanist Archaeologists (SAfA) organized the society's biennial conference around the issues of looting and destruction of Africa's material and cultural past. He went on to organize a Carter Lecture Series in April 1993 at the University of Florida to revisit the major issues and themes that had arisen there. Delegates were invited from across Africa and from Mexico and the US to give further perspectives on the problems under discussion. The subsequent publication, *Plundering Africa's Past,* marked a landmark event in our understanding and appreciation of the scale of the concerns (Schmidt & McIntosh 1996). At the same time Susan Keech McIntosh, who has done so much to develop archaeology in West Africa, published two insightful and progressive relevant articles (McIntosh 1992; 1993). In both she demonstrated the major problems facing the funding and resourcing of archaeological practice and suggested that the World Bank should engage in capacity building in this subject area. This, it was proposed, should be linked with a programme of surveys and national inventories to allow proper management and curation strategies to be put in place.

Indeed, the World Bank and a range of other organizations and institutions have increasingly recognized the linkages between archaeology and development. While UNESCO has of course been the primary advocate for work in this area, other organizations have also been proactive. Government departments (in particular the development agencies of a number of Scandinavian countries), foundations like those of the Aga Khan and Ford, NGOs including the World Monuments Fund and Global Heritage Fund have all been key players in this arena. This work is not without its problems, as we shall see in later chapters, but it has also been witness to some major achievements, significant advances and innovative schemes.

One of the most important initiatives over the past two decades began to take shape in 1996. That year an initial assessment of conservation practice and the state of immovable heritage in Africa was conducted across 44 countries. Subsequently in 1998 at a meeting in Côte d'Ivoire the AFRICA 2009 programme was launched. Its primary objective was to increase national capacity in sub-Saharan Africa for the management and conservation of immovable cultural heritage and involved a partnership between the UNESCO World Heritage Centre, ICCROM, and various national African cultural heritage agencies, CraTerre-EAG, EPA and CHDA. Funding was supplied by a number of Scandinavian governments and agencies, the Italian government, the World Heritage Fund and ICCROM. Some private finance was also made available. The programme is ongoing and has had varied success. Further commentary on this major initiative will be found in later chapters.

In 2001, eleven years after SAfA's 1990 conference, a one-day seminar on *Safeguarding Africa's Archaeological Past* was held at the School of Oriental and African Studies at the University of London (Finneran 2005). The programme examined issues ranging from management, museum provision, conservation and ethics. Amongst the seminar's objectives included an attempt to publicize the issues facing heritage protection in Africa and examining mechanisms with which the situation could be improved. The issue of looting had not gone away, and if anything the problems facing the continent were even greater in terms of broader institutional capacity.

While debate has only emerged recently within the discipline of archaeology about its role in society and its potential role in development other subject areas have been engaged in this form of internal dialogue for decades. Anthropology underwent a major period of introspection throughout the later 1960s and 1970s. By the closing decades of the twentieth century anthropologists had come to recognize the potentially powerful set of forces and techniques they could bring to effect change in society. Early on they engaged with the emergent development paradigms and provided input into their formative theoretical phases. Such pro-active approaches were exemplified in Gardner and Lewis's 1996 *Anthropology, Development and the Post-Modern Challenge*, in which the authors advocated a strong inclusive voice for anthropology in developmental practice and policy. Archaeology, by contrast, has been a largely insular subject with an antiquated and academy-orientated approach to its own exclusive interests. This insularity is slowly breaking down, but one of the key aims of this volume is to encourage further inclusiveness, greater questioning of the value of the subject and a movement towards integrated approaches to environment, development and society. This approach has already been taken up by Jeremy Sabloff of the University of Pennsylvania Museum, who has challenged archaeologists to move beyond simply generating understandings of the past to facilitate bringing about change and making a difference in contemporary society (Sabloff 2008).

It is also worth noting that within the broader sphere of cultural studies linkages have been made with development approaches. Most notably from a UK university perspective, Professor John Mack at the University of East Anglia has developed an innovative masters course on cultural heritage and international development. Such advances are greatly welcomed and should go some way towards producing a new generation of researchers and practitioners in this area.

Structure of the book

This introduction has outlined the primary research context of this volume and briefly addressed a number of directly relevant previous studies.

Chapter 2 provides a definitional context, examining in greater depth a number of the dominant existing paradigms governing this work and addressing the primary concepts used. It should be stressed that many of these analyses are subjective readings. Most of the concepts are contested and rather than present an overview of generalized opinion we felt that a more personal perspective would be valuable. Numerous publications deal with the various approaches to these concepts and the reader is directed to the bibliography in order to explore these more fully.

Chapter 3 presents an overview of the primary issues affecting the archaeological resource in Africa over the past twenty years. It also examines in more detail the specific threats that face the resource today. Of course the resource in the continent is not unique in being exposed to such a wide range of threats, but it does exist in a unique socio-economic and political environment. The protection of and investment in such a resource could justifiably be seen as a less pressing problem than the issues of poverty, hunger and war, but when we contextualize archaeology within the broader framework of the environment and its constituent resources we will see that we cannot simply ignore it and that its protection can be a positive force for change.

Chapter 4 provides a generalized overview of contemporary cultural resource management (CRM) or cultural heritage management (CHM) practice across Africa. One of the problems with writing about Africa is the varying dynamics and diversity of the continent. Things are constantly changing, governments come and go, countries can swing widely through perceived success and supposed failure. Some of the observations in this chapter may not chime with readers who have a particular expertise and knowledge of specific countries, but the chapter is necessarily generalist and serves to paint a broad picture of varying practice and resource levels.

Chapter 5 examines the international legislative and agency context for facilitating and promoting conservation and management practice of the archaeological resource. It addresses the role and general operation of the myriad of international, governmental and non-governmental organizations involved in this work across Africa.

Chapter 6 begins to engage with current international development practice and looks at a number of ways in which archaeology can contribute to the major themes and issues affecting contemporary practice. A number of major concerns underlie and drive current thinking in this broad field, and archaeologists can and should contribute to debates over climate and environment change, the development and expansion of capitalism and globalization, colonial practice and general change in human society.

Chapter 7 looks at specific projects that are contributing to the aforementioned arguments and examines a number of specific strategies with which archaeology can inform programmes aimed at environmental sustainability, poverty alleviation and advocacy.

Finally, Chapter 8 presents a series of thoughts on how archaeology can engage and integrate into future international development practice. It also outlines a number of potential initiatives that could be undertaken to further enhance protection, involve communities, improve government and university practice and develop capacity.

2

Definitions and concepts

One of the major issues facing the contemporary academy and professional sphere is the singularity and insularity of single discipline work. Researchers and practitioners rarely, if ever, venture outside their specialist fields, and multidisciplinarity often remains only an aspiration. This polarity is probably most pronounced between the earth and biological sciences, and the social sciences and humanities. Consequently development theory will rarely feature among the academic concerns of scientists working in areas as diverse as microbiology to landscape formation and hazard mapping. There may be a vague appreciation that their work has broader uses, but this transference and policy application is left to others to implement. This absence of dedicated holistic 'development teams' is regrettable and is ultimately detrimental to development practice as a whole. Similarly, the linkage between development and the cultural heritage resource is a much neglected subject area. UNESCO has recently advocated a far stronger connection, and some of the latest published work coming from this organization is to be welcomed and encouraged. However, in the context of this publication it is necessary to provide a definitional context and framework for the concepts, approaches and terminology used. A number of these may subsequently appear over-generalist, but they are written in the hope that researchers and practitioners with a variety of backgrounds and training might read this volume and find sections of it useful. Many of these are contested spheres, so an attempt will be made to address the varied approaches taken and meanings advocated for the different views presented.

Tangible and intangible heritage

Heritage is a complex term and one that can too easily be approached from a simplistic structuralist perspective. At its simplest, tangible heritage consists of the physical remains of past societies, including sites, monuments, landscapes and artefacts. These remain as strong visible connectors to the past with which most sectors of society will be familiar, and it is these archaeological remains with which we are most concerned in this volume. However, heritage can also be less tangible and can include music, language and ritual. UNESCO's 2003 *Convention for the Safeguarding of Intangible Cultural Heritage* defines ICH as the practices, representations, expressions, knowledge and skills that communities, groups and, in some cases, individuals recognize as part of their cultural heritage. It can include oral traditions and expressions, including language, performing arts; social practices, rituals and festive events; knowledge and practices concerning nature and the universe and traditional craftsmanship.

Heritage places can also be sacred places, points in the landscape that may not have a monumental presence but nonetheless are special. Woodland, rock outcrops and even particular places at sea can all be special places filled with meaning for specific communities or individuals. Heritage can also be more abstract. It can relate to one's perceptions of inheritance or a shared past. Community traditions and practice are an integral part of this. It can define and interpret identity and be used to legitimize or justify power and systems of hierarchy (Skeates 2000: 9). Heritage cannot then be selective, it has to be inclusive. It cannot just deal with the 'best' or the most significant achievements of past societies but must be truly reflective of all facets of past activities and undertakings. Heritage should maintain past collective experience and become a formative process for contemporary society in learning from past failure, and indeed success. Heritage should also be inclusive of all facets of society and not just be concerned with inanimate objects or buildings detached from meaning or experience. Often this interpretation of heritage has led to commodification and leads heritage components to be part of the cultural tourist product. While recognizing the consequent duality of heritage linked to economic and cultural capital (Graham et al. 2000: 23), it cannot become an exclusive commodity. Heritage requires multi-vocality not only in its formation and interpretation but also in its participation and appreciation. Access to heritage and participation in heritage-related activity must be fully representational. We also recognize that heritage is not a static process but one that is continually developing and adapting. Heritage is a constant that takes full cognizance of the past, integrates into the present and recognizes and anticipates a future.

Heritage has then assumed a range of meanings and definitions and there are as many approaches to heritage as there are practitioners. Heritage can be defined as 'the contemporary use of the past' (Graham et al. 2000: 2) in that it creates a connection with the past and allows us to construct contemporary perspectives on the past in order to develop a sense of who and what we currently are. Heritage then creates a sense of belonging and is an integral part of how we perceive ourselves and develop identity.

Heritage, culture and ethnicity

Definitions of both culture and ethnicity are in themselves complex and contested (Allen 2000). A basic interpretation of what culture is could be 'the beliefs, values and lifeways of people within their perceived society and sense of place'. Culture then is not something that is biologically inherited or passed through genes. Instead it is learned and consists of a series of memories and interpretations of contemporary generations adopted from ancestors, associates or community. It is also an active rather than a passive process, continually changing and adapting to particular needs and responsibilities. Ethnicity constitutes an extension of this identification of values and norms. Cultural and ethnic responses to contemporary society and its inherent processes such as the continued expansion of globalization are varied and complex, ranging from increased cultural uniformity to cultural empowerment and a rise in cultural identity.

Ethnicity and identity

It is easy to throw around words like ethnicity and identity, but their actual definitions vary greatly among academic practitioners. In general ethnic groups are defined by (and define themselves by) ascriptive differences, including those of language, religion, colour, concepts of origin and descent, historical experience and cultural traits (Hanlon 2006a: 95). Archaeology can be a key tool in elucidating the development of contemporary identities and has additionally shown that ethnicity can also be marked by food styles, household arrangements, and dress and ornament (Meskell 2001: 190). Ethnicity often makes reference to commonalities, such as shared historical understandings and contemporary cultural traditions across particular groups. The key here is how groups shape and form their relative identities. This is often politically loaded and based on created or artificial boundaries. The consequent construct of identity and ethnicity is thus hugely complex and often contested. It is a fluid process, never static. The changing and renegotiation of identity, culminating in the recent past in the upsurge of nationalistic movements across Europe, have marked much of human history.

One of the most obvious expressions of this, for example, was the creation of a pan-Celtic identity in the nineteenth century, produced out of a romantic movement based on pseudo-science and limited evidence. More recently the political development of the European Union has seen the growth of Pan-European research and a marked bias toward a shared European heritage, creating for many an academic environment in which material cultural linkages have been over-extended in light of prevailing funding orientations. A similar construct of ethnicity resulted in the emergence of many of the European nationalist movements in the nineteenth century and was arguably a contributory factor to the outbreak of both world wars. This can be a loaded and politically dangerous undertaking: witness Hitler's use of archaeology to legitimize his understandings and aspirations for the Aryan race. Similar examples can be drawn from an African context, notably at Great Zimbabwe where much effort was put into ascribing a European or Near Eastern ancestry to it and its associated monuments.

Ethnicity and conflict

Ethnicity has consistently been put forward as one of the underlying causes of conflict and war through the ages. In contemporary times Hanlon (2006a: 95) has noted that both George Bush and Bill Clinton ascribed ethnic origins to the conflict in the Balkans. Similarly there is a widespread assumption that ethnicity has constituted a major factor in previous decades of conflict and civil war across Africa and elsewhere. However, the degree to which identity-related issues lead to conflict is one of the most contentious matters facing the development community today. Researchers, when addressing the extent to which ethnicity plays a part in the outbreak of conflict and war, fall broadly into two camps. Primordialists argue that ethnicity is innate and fixed and as a result the rivalry between ethnic groups has long sustained conflict and often leads to war. The second group, commonly called constructivists, see identity and aspects of ethnicity as a constantly changing phenomenon. This process is often manipulated by power groups in society to maintain the *status quo*, effect change and often introduce conflict. Importantly, DfID (2001), in a report on the causes of conflict in Africa, noted that 'ethnic conflict has increasingly been sanctioned or exploited to gain support for the continuation of the conflict' on a regional basis. The report goes on to state that ethnicity, often based on artificial creations, is abused by both political leaders and belligerents to advance their particular cause or power base. Much of this violence is located within specific national areas, but it is increasingly spreading across borders, for example the current situation in Darfur, affecting the Sudan, Chad and the Central African Republic. A number of these conflicts have been labelled civil war, defined here as a war 'mainly within one country and where fighting is primarily between people of that country' (Hanlon 2006b, 46). This is a contentious term, given the subjectivity with which many people approach particular situations. What might be viewed as a justifiable insurrection by one person may be seen as mindless misdirected violence by another. The International Committee of the Red Cross (ICRC) makes reference to armed conflicts which are not of an international nature but 'generally refer to conflicts with armed forces on either side which are in many respects similar to an international war, but take place within the confines of a single country' (ICRC 2005).

While ethnicity is cited repeatedly as a causative factor in conflict on the African continent, closer more informed study recognizes that the majority of tribal and group identities in sub-Saharan African have been created over the last 200 years through internal migrations and movement. Colonial powers were extensively engaged in this process in an effort to categorize and control society. As a consequence we see the artificial construction of bi-tribal identity in Rwanda with the meaningless labelling of Hutu and Tutsi peoples by the Belgian colonial power, an assignation of cultural affiliation which was later to have devastating consequences. Across Africa archaeology can play a part in creating more nuanced understandings of identity construction to help develop greater understandings between peoples and groupings. This will be developed further in Chapter **7**.

Archaeology and built cultural heritage

There are nearly as many definitions of what archaeology is as there are practitioners in the field. Most definitions, however, are limiting, and include the study of past material culture and structures. Most definitions will also focus on the physicality of the past, for example UNESCO's description of tangible cultural heritage as including movable cultural heritage (paintings, sculptures, coins, manuscripts, etc.), immovable cultural heritage (monuments, archaeological sites, and so on) and underwater cultural heritage (shipwrecks, underwater ruins and cities and so on). But the subject area is far wider than simply the examination of artefactual material from the past. It also includes the study of landscapes and the interaction between humans and the natural world in all its manifestations. Not only does archaeology study societies but it also examines past environments, investigates past lifeways and develops understanding of cultural processes. Ultimately archaeology is the science of examining past peoples and the world they lived in. How this examination actually takes place is hugely varied and ranges from the large-scale mapping of landscapes with the use of remote sensing through to individual site survey and excavation. Archaeology will also draw from a range of other disciplines to aid in its investigations, including physical anthropology, forensic science, flora and fauna analysis, architecture, history, geology and geomorphology. It is a highly integrated and inclusive subject area that attempts to create holistic understandings of the past. Mostly it focuses on the story of past peoples and the way they lived, worked, thought and died.

Cultural resource management (CRM)

Broadly speaking CRM is the professional practice of the identification, examination, management and protection of cultural resources. It is an inclusive term that incorporates the physical remains of the past including movable and immovable heritage such as monuments, sites and artefacts, supported by a range of legislation, government policy and professional practice. It can also consider issues associated with identity, ideology and agency. Increasingly landscapes are also viewed as multifaceted cultural entities closely aligned to natural heritage and societal development. Places of spiritual or religious value as well as community practices and traditions can equally be regarded as cultural resources. The view that archaeology constitutes both an environmental landscape resource and a cultural resource is integral to the adoption of this terminology. It recognizes the non-renewable nature of much of the resource and its relative fragility in the face of an ever-changing world. This fragility and range of threats has lead to the development of a burgeoning professional industry around the resource. The actual practice of CRM ranges from the physical protection and interpretation of resources through to their investigation, preservation and often enhancement. Practitioners will also engage in educational awareness programmes and the dissemination of resource information to the broader society. The term enjoys widest usage in the USA, where it encompasses the arts and heritage (Knudson 1999). It is commonly associated with heritage and more specifically with the archaeological resource, although conservation architects and architectural historians also employ the term. In the UK, Ireland and across Europe the term 'heritage management' or Cultural Heritage Management (CHM) is more frequently used. In other countries this terminology has political connotations. Australia replaced 'resource' with 'heritage' in the 1990s following criticisms from the aboriginal community that the term 'resource' implied equal access by and identification with all the population, and did not recognize that the indigenous peoples claimed a single heritage and special relationship with certain places and material culture (Smith 2004: 6).

International development

International development is a contested term and one that has given risen to significant debate. Four approaches to the use of the word 'development' have been forwarded by Thomas (2001) and Gasper (2004). These include development as a driver for fundamental or structural change, development as an interventionist strategy to bring about change, development as improvement, and development as creating the basis for improvement. Alan Thomas (2000: 43) has proposed four primary perspectives on development processes in the context of the international alleviation of poverty through various forms of development. If one accepts development as an immanent process within capitalism then one approaches the concept from a neo-liberal perspective, laying special emphasis on market expansion and economic development. Closely aligned to this is the role of individuals as entrepreneurs acting as the primary agents for developing profit-driven ventures, economic entities and emergent economic activity as the key to the alleviation of poverty. International development can then be seen in some instances as creating 'obstacles' to the market (ibid.). This approach to free market economics has been a dominant paradigm over the past decades, one of course that has recently been shown to be both morally corrupt and prone to total collapse.

Another approach is to recognize the parallel relationship between capitalism and development, but here there is an awareness of the inherent problems within contemporary capitalism. This school looks at ways in which greater market efficiency and aspects of governance can be improved to help ease the burden of poverty. A degree of intervention by both internal and external agencies is then often welcomed. A third perspective emerges from the movement against capitalism, which aspires to a more socially led egalitarianism that empowers the so-called lower classes and communities. Economics may not play such a central role in this process as empowerment may lay differing emphases on attainment and personal 'wealth'. Aligned to this is the concept of alternative development, or populist bottom-up development, where change for good is centred on societal participation often led by NGOs or community-based organizations. This perspective could be viewed as a structuralist approach, which lays emphasis on economics, seeing it in the context of historical struggle between differing social classes (Thomas 2000: 44). A distinctly Marxist perspective often underlies this, and both Dependency Theory and a World Systems approach have emerged as a result. The former Brazilian President Fernando Henrique Cardoso (1969) has been one of the foremost writers on dependency and centre and periphery relationships, while Immanuel Wallerstein (1974; 1980) labelled it the 'World System'. Both recognize the intrinsic inequalities of the global economic system where a core-periphery relationship exists. Here the key resources, both natural and human, flow from the poorer periphery regions to the central core 'developed' nations. Historically this relationship was established through the colonial and imperialist activities of European countries. In the contemporary world the Global North countries maintain a relationship of dependency through military might, media, trade restrictions and agreements, and controls over the geopolitical arena.

Through this relationship of control, countries outside the Global North are made to react to 'world market conditions' before they are homogenized into the system. This occurs through a combination of both internal and external drivers. Politically, the creation of larger less locally-oriented decision-making units in Africa, while acting to try to balance internal autonomy, has created a subservience to world-market conditions. Technologically, Africa's ability to acquire and control the elements necessary for production is also controlled by the Global North as a result of the inequalities of the European Industrial Revolution and subsequent colonial activities. This has directly resulted in the Global South lacking adequate economic capital to compete equally within the capitalist world system, while those individuals and states within the Global South who are seemingly able to control production have been permitted, aided and often subsidized by institutions from the North. Ultimately, to ensure compatibility with the world system African states must create a secure institutional infrastructure and currency (Wallerstein 1989: 130-1), an outcome arguably impossible due to the political and economic world system and its intrinsic inequalities outlined here. A radical renegotiation of Africa's place in the world and the world's attitude toward it is therefore needed – a renegotiation that can begin with the development of African (and by reflection global) identities based upon an understanding of the past.

Finally, in post-development thinking a rejectionist view of most forms of development and international aid exists. This school has developed critiques of most forms of interventionism, but encompasses a variety of thinkers ranging from neo-Marxists to free market economists who favour the natural progress of capitalism. The latter group see capitalism and its associated economic components as primary agents of evolving and varied development. Some radical thinkers oppose contemporary development from different perspectives, seeing it as a form of neo-colonialism and a Western construct. This contested approach is evident in the writings of Arturo Escobar who describes development as a set of ideas and practices that functions as a mechanism for colonial and neo-colonial control over the South by the North (Escobar 1995: 26-39). An intrinsic part of this process is the search for new markets rooted in capitalist practice. He also criticized anthropologists for failing to question development as a construct that seeks to order and control the world (Gardner & Lewis 1996).

Ultimately academics can theorize about division and approach in an exclusive removed environment but global problems remain. Debate will continue but engagement must also take place. Allen and Thomas (2000) use the concept of development working to bring about 'good change' while Potter et al. (2008: 6) forward a working definition, stating that 'development is change … for better or for worse … that is intended to lead to the betterment of people and places around the globe'. Both are useful approaches. It is recognized here that there are considerable problems and issues facing the development field but there is also a strong ethical argument that contemporary society must at least engage with inequality and disparity across the North/South divide and develop a dialogue that examines the causes of these differences and works at ways to bring about better or good change.

3

Issues and threats

It is unsurprising that across the African continent the archaeological resource is under significant pressure. Given the centuries of political turmoil, conflict, environmental degradation and poverty, the protection of the archaeological resource has received little attention. Few systematic studies have been undertaken into the vulnerability of the resource, but some insights have been gained from more generalized analysis and through a limited number of specific projects. At the August 2002 World Summit on Sustainable Development a parallel event was held examining World Heritage in Africa and its inherent linkage with sustainable development (UNESCO 2002). The subsequent *Johannesburg Declaration* recognized that the World Heritage Sites in Africa faced threats from war and environmental degradation, coupled with poor or absent management. UNESCO analysis suggested that 25% of World Heritage Sites in danger were in Africa. Four years later in 2006, 43% of the global sites classified as World Heritage in Danger under Article 11 (4) of the Convention were located in Africa (http://whc.unesco.org/en/danger/). Of course these figures are only representative of the limited number of designated World Heritage Sites, so in reality the actual percentage of sites under threat throughout Africa is far higher.

Across Africa the cultural and built heritage resource is subject to a complex set of processes which serve to undermine not only its structural and archaeological integrity but also its place and potential role within society. The range of threats impacting upon the resource can be broadly grouped into four categories. Each of these factors overlaps with the other catego-

Fig. 5. Vegetation at the medieval town of Gedi, Kenya.

ries, creating a complex web of socio-political and environmental elements coming together to undermine the integrity
and sustainability of the resource (Fig. 5):

1. Political neglect and institutional capacity;
2. Environment and climate change;
3. Illicit trade and looting;
4. Commercial/development pressures.

Political neglect and institutional capacity

The most complex factor is the negative resource impacts generated through public and civic society. The majority of African countries have received little if any funding for the protection and management of the archaeological resource. This is hardly surprising given the state of society across the continent over the past 60 years. A country which has undergone periodic states of internal and external war and has lurched from one food crisis to another will hardly give financial priority to preserving archaeological sites and monuments. Even relatively stable countries are not in a position to fund such enterprise to the extent that is needed. Where conservation has taken place, it has often been carried out in an unsympathetic and unsustainable manner. The process of state-building is complex, with health, education and infrastructure justifiably taking priority over cultural resource protection. Nevertheless, there are good reasons for prioritizing cultural heritage at an early stage of state-building. These have been addressed throughout this volume and include economic, environmental and social values.

Limited management capacity, coupled in a number of instances with poor governance, poses one of the most fundamental threats to individual sites and their broader contextual preservation frameworks. The current instability under the Mugabe regime in Zimbabwe, for example, has already prevented researchers from continuing work on the cultural landscape surrounding Great Zimbabwe, and the massive inflation within the country has meant that heritage provision is now very low on the government's agenda. Continued regional instability in certain countries and the increasing transboundary nature of these conflicts is also posing a threat to future site protection. Areas such as the DRC, eastern Chad,

Darfur and Somalia are no longer safe or accessible to researchers. With archaeology and cultural heritage featuring so low in government priority a number of key issues have emerged. Institutional capacity and limited, if indeed any, resources pose a major problem. If government will and support is wanting then the ability to establish and sustain institutions such as state heritage agencies and museums becomes very difficult. Even where such agencies are established they are often ineffective or lack sufficient expertise or finances to develop sustainable heritage management programmes. The limited nature and availability of inventories across Africa is systematic of this lack of support and direction (McIntosh 1993). Coupled with restricted implementation of environmental assessment legislation and strategies and constrained input into the development and planning process, this has reduced the archaeological resource and its managers to an insignificant role. A number of countries, such as South Africa, do have a better record in this regard, but even in Egypt with its incredible treasures little cognisance is given to rescue or development archaeology.

Environment and climate change

The process of rapid and unprecedented climate change is now accepted. Current predictions see temperature rising by anything up to 7° in high emission models with consequent changes to rainfall levels, marked sea-level rise and increased pressure on water supplies. Further, the effects on human populations include worries about future food security, widespread displacement and increased incidences of vector-borne diseases (IPCC 2001). It is evident that these natural processes and rapid environmental change will pose a primary, but still largely unquantifiable threat, to the archaeological resource. This has been recognized by senior heritage professionals including Achim Steiner, UN Under-Secretary General and UNEP Executive Director, who has stated that the global community must use scientific knowledge to 'assist managers of culturally important sites like buildings and archaeological finds. Losses here as a result of climate change may impact on the livelihoods of local people and, especially in developing countries, add to poverty' (ICOMOS 2007: 192). The World Heritage Committee (2006) has put forward a useful evaluation of key areas of concern when it comes to the impacts of climate change over the coming decades. They include the perceived stability of buried material once the natural balance of sediment is disturbed due to structural change associated with physical, chemical or biological alteration; increases in soil moisture and greater degrees of salt mobilization; increases in pest infestation of organic building materials; an increase in flooding and greater structural damage due to more frequent and strong storm events; and movable heritage will be subject to increased temperature and UV exposure. Finally, specific concern is raised over the spectre of population displacement and upheaval leading to the loss of traditional lifeways and the movement of communities away from cultural sites. In addition ICOMOS (2007: 193) has highlighted the economic impacts associated with changing patterns of cultural tourism and associated consequences for intangible heritage, landscapes and traditional building skills; impacts associated with freeze/thaw on building materials; and structural damage resulting from differential sediment settling and soil compaction due to changes in ground water levels. The World Heritage Committee (2006) has identified the specific parameters affecting cultural heritage, including temperature change, atmospheric moisture change, sea-level rise, wind, desertification, pollution and biological infestation.

Specifically, macro-processes such as desertification and coastal erosion intrinsically linked to a rapidly changing global environment are the primary sources of gradual destruction at sites like Kilwa Kisiwani and Songo Mnara in Tanzania and the Royal Palaces of Abomey in Benin. At Kilwa Kisiwani, an eleventh- to seventeenth-century historic port town (Chittick 1974), significant sections of the foreshore are subject to erosion linked with changing sea levels and shifting beach profiles. Recent cutting of littoral mangrove is accelerating this process, which is not helped by an increase in commercial development along the coast. While this process has accelerated over the past century, clear evidence of sea-level rise can be found across much of East and West Africa and the Red Sea with archaeological sites providing key indicators of change. Many countries in West and Central Africa are especially susceptible to this change due to the low-lying lagoonal-coasts (IPCC 2001). In particular a considerable part of the Nile Delta will be lost to both inundation and erosion. The historic waterfront and harbour at Alexandria is especially susceptible to this change and has been subject to extensive sea-defence campaigns over the past 20 years.

Other processes are directly impacting on a series of World Heritage Sites. In 1984 a tornado initially damaged the royal palace site of Aborney, Benin, a series of palaces dating from 1625 to 1900 contained within a cob-wall area (Joffroy & Moriset 1995; 1996). Since then a continuous threat comes during the rainy season, when roofs have the potential to collapse and undermine the earthen walls. Other threats include termite and insect attack, although a number of international conservation programmes have been initiated to stabilize and enhance the site. The general pattern of climate change has an intrinsic role in each of these processes. Deterioration and structural problems with the three great mosques at Timbuktu, Mali have been linked to desertification (Sidi 2006). The Chinguetti Mosque in Mauritania has also been identified as being at specific risk from the advance and accretion of sands (World Heritage Committee 2006). Other sites similarly threatened include a number of Meroe sites in Sudan and a number of pyramid sites across Egypt.

Illicit trade and looting

The effective rape of cultural treasures from many African countries has its origins in the colonial period. With the exploration and expansion of European countries into the continent intense interest emerged in the historical past of a number of countries. This was especially true in Egypt and the African countries bordering the Mediterranean. No such interest was shown in the historical past of the sub-Saharan countries, their populations being viewed as primitive and lacking in cultural sophistication. As we have seen, even when clear physical evidence existed of an impressive urban or monumental past, such as that at Great Zimbabwe, it was dismissed as being of external origin and unrelated to an indigenous African past. By contrast, the monumentality of ancient Egypt and Nubia and the classical ruins of Libya provoked intense study across Western Europe. A cultural scramble to obtain examples of these artefacts erupted between museums and institutions. Collection rivalry between the great cultural houses for these antiquities reflected the geopolitics of the time and mirrored the military rivalry between their respective countries. Major European institutions still hold these collections and there is little talk of repatriation. While these initial collection policies were couched in early academic justificatory terms, looting and twentieth-century collecting was organized on the basis of monetary greed and criminality. Brodie (2005) describes a 'western fetish for tribal art' emerging in the early part of the last century. Originating in the antiquarianism of the nine-teenth century, a commercial market had emerged for African material through the 1920s and 30s. A hiatus had been reached in the sale of masks and ritual paraphernalia by the 1950s and the market had shifted to more utilitarian objects (Brodie 2005: 23). In particular a series of figures and terracottas from West Africa became valuable collectables in the later decades of the century. Figures from Djenné in Mali had been known since the nineteenth century, but were not exhibited until 1970, in Zurich. Their monetary value rose as a consequence and a major trade developed. McIntosh (1996: 46) suggests that be-fore 1977 possibly thousands of terracottas were looted from Djenné. This was a well organized systematic stripping of cul-tural assets, the organization of which appeared to stretch all the way to the presidential office in Mali. An extensive network emerged in this trade, from the farmers and organized plunder-ers up to go-between antique dealers in Africa's towns to the collectors, dealers, galleries and museums of Europe and North America (Sidibé 1996, 83).

A similar phenomenon occurred following the display of the Bura statuettes from Niger, uncovered in 1983 and displayed at an international exhibition across West Africa and France between 1993-98. Significant looting took place at their origin sites following their display (Brodie 2005). It is suggested that in the Nok area European dealers organized systematic looting for terracottas in 1983, an activity that continued for many years with over a thousand people engaged in looting by 1995 (Brodie 2005: 24). Elsewhere in the region of Dia, part of the inland Niger Delta area in Mali, 80% of archaeological sites in 2000 had been subject to some level of looting in the search for 'Djenné-style' terracotta (MacDonald 2005: 34).

The impact of looting at African archaeological sites and the associated illicit antiquities trade has received significant attention over the past twenty years (Finneran 2005; Schmidt & McIntosh 1996). The individuals who highlighted the extent of these activities have done a valuable service to the international community in revealing the criminality and destructiveness of this trade. As a consequence of their actions there is an increased awareness of the damage these activities cause and their wider impact among communities across the continent. Much of the well documented looting has occurred in West Africa, but there are many other countries across the continent that have been subject to looting on a more reduced scale. The exceptions are episodic events such as the ransacking and thorough looting of the National Museum in Mogadishu in 1991 and the loss of ethnographic collections from the Hargeysa Museum in Northern Somalia during that country's civil war (Schmidt & McIntosh 1996: 8). The Italians had established a museum in Mogadishu in 1933 with 3,500 artefacts listed in 1934. The institution subsequently became the National Museum after independence in 1960 (Brandt & Mohamed 1996: 252).

Other forms of organized looting include the trade in rock art. The site of Imaoun has been plundered with pieces sold to tourists while similar activity has also occurred at Adrar where rocks have been used for building purposes (Larocca 2005: 29). In Algeria hundreds of engravings and paintings have been removed from historic rock faces at Tassilli n-Ajjer, a World Heritage Site, and at Hoggar. While professional thieves have been partly responsible for this, a number of politically motivated Islamic groups have also played a part. Some looting in effect achieves government sanction. The government of Mozambique has licensed a treasure hunting company, Arqueonautas Worldwide, S.A. to explore the waters off the World Heritage Site of Isle de Mozambique for profit. This company previously exploited the waters of Cape Verde and is actively looking at ways of expanding its enterprise across Africa.

One of the more innovative responses to illicit trade came in 1997 following an Amsterdam workshop organized by ICOM (International Council of Museums) on the Protection of the African Cultural Heritage. In an attempt to move towards a common response to the threats posed by the trade, the participants drew up a list of categories of African archaeological objects deemed at particular risk. The so-called Red List includes the following artefact categories.

Artefact category	Geographical location
Nok terracotta	Bauchi Plateau and the Katsina and Sokoto regions (Nigeria)
Terracotta and bronzes	Ife (Nigeria)
Esie stone statues	(Nigeria)
Terracotta, bronzes and pottery	Niger Valley (Mali)
Terracotta statuettes, bronzes, potteries, and stone statues	Bura System (Niger, Burkina Faso)
Stone statues	North of Burkina Faso and neighbouring regions
Terracotta	North of Ghana (Komaland) and Côte d'Ivoire
Terracotta and bronzes	'Sao' (Cameroon, Chad, Nigeria)

Table 3.1. ICOM Red list of artefact categories at risk, 1997.

3. Issues and threats

Development pressures

UNESCO (2003: 47) reported that in 2002 84% of World Heritage Sites in Africa had their visual integrity threatened. The structural integrity of 26 of the cultural sites was threatened by a combination of road and factory building, erosion and pollution, while 83% of them were under threat from natural catastrophes including fire, flooding pollution and deforestation.

Urban development

Many cities throughout sub-Saharan Africa are witnessing rapid expansion associated with displaced internal populations and commercial growth led by both entrepreneurial activity and multinational expansion. Such development invariably has an effect on both built and buried cultural heritage with, for example, the extensive linear earthworks at Benin City in Nigeria, a candidate site for World Heritage designation, being under intensive pressure from urban expansion and land grabbing activity. Similar pressures are present at Mombasa in Kenya where a number of sites with high archaeological potential within the island's historic urban core have been cordoned off illegally for present and future development.

Unsympathetic commercial and tourism development is also affecting the coastline surrounding Zanzibar Stone Town and Isle de Mozambique. Zanzibar Stone Town physically represents one of the most culturally dynamic and ethnically diverse settlements across the southern hemisphere. Its fusion of African, Arabic, Indian and European architectural styles and human experience represents over 800 years of development and expansion from the time the town originated as a fishing village as early as the eleventh century AD (Sherriff 1987; Gilbert 2004). It was subsequently witness to numerous reconfigurations as various groups and powers exerted a physical presence, from initial Portuguese colonization in the sixteenth century to later Omani control. The vast majority of the standing buildings in the old part of the town, centred on the

Shangani peninsula, have been constructed over the last 200 years. These buildings were for the most part owned by the Arab mercantile elite, but following the revolution of 1964 many changed ownership. It has been suggested that of the 1,709 buildings in Stone Town, approximately 75% are deteriorating (Sherriff 1995). In fact all the buildings are in varying states of decay linked to population pressures. Specifically, Stone Town has attracted ever-increasing population numbers drawn from the rural hinterland in search of employment. Poorer groups paying low rent have turned many of the large historic buildings into tenements with many of their pre-1964 owners waiving their ownership rights, following traditional Islamic practice, to facilitate occupation by these groups. As a result sympathetic conservation is virtually absent. Similarly there is little in the way of centralized government control and protection for the old town. The various policies and plans that have been put in place have mostly failed and the conservation that has taken place is largely inadequate. One possible exception is the work of the Aga Khan Foundation in restoring the old dispensary building.

Tourism

Development pressures are associated not only with the development of industry and commerce but also with tourist infrastructure. Archaeological sites have become an integral part of the tourist experience across Africa. This is exemplified by the pivotal role ancient remains play in the economy and identity of Egypt. There is an acceptance that tourism, managed properly, can contribute positively to community, but it has also the potential to impact negatively on the cultural resource. Visitor numbers, the exclusion of local community, the commodification and creation of exclusive space and the introduction of contentious cultural practices can all have a negative influence on built heritage remains. These processes have been more apparent at World Heritage Sites, given their high international profile. The threat to such sites from increasingly higher tourist numbers has been documented both in Africa and else-

Fig. 6. Visitors at the Giza pyramids, Egypt.

where across the globe (Nadeau 2006). The commodification and alteration of many residential and mercantile buildings in Stone Town and at James Island, Gambia, are reflective of this process. Widespread proliferation of souvenir and trinket shops, restaurants and other outlets remains largely unchecked, exacerbates cultural division and widens the economic gap between the indigenous poor and relatively wealthy tourist. Increasing tourist numbers at the sacred landscapes at Tsodilo and uKhahlamba in South Africa have the potential to contribute to this cultural dichotomy and reduction of traditionalist beliefs to Western attractions. Six of the cultural World Heritage Sites across sub-Saharan Africa have reported that their visitor numbers are unsustainable and have put undue pressure on the individual sites (UNESCO 2003: 50). Two of these, Great Zimbabwe and the Island of Gorée, have in excess of 100,000 visitors a year. Tourism at Isle de Mozambique has also led to illicit artefact trading. Large numbers of displaced and poverty stricken youth earn a living from selling artefacts to Western visitors. Tourism numbers have also had an impact on a number of high profile sites across Egypt (Fig. 6). The walls of the tomb of Seti I have been damaged through tourist contact while septic tank leakages into the Valley of the Kings tomb 5 and exhaust fumes have exaggerated the rate of decay (Skeates 2000: 61).

Globalization

Many of the above issues could be grouped under the general process of contemporary globalization, a complex and contested phenomenon with numerous associated definitions and under-standings. Most agree that it is related to the concept of an ever-shrinking world linked to global economic, political and cultural interconnectedness (McGrew 2000: 346). Palmer (2004: 3), offering a neo-capitalist perspective, defines globali-zation as the diminution of state-enforced restrictions on vol-untary exchange across borders and the increasingly integrated and complex global system of exchange and produc-tion. Globalization can then be intrinsically linked to the global capitalist movement designed to move, promote and ultimately sell goods. It is seen here as being primarily related to the trans-national nature and increased uniformity and availabil-ity of material goods, access to travel and the gradual emer-gence of a one-world capitalist economic system – all propagated through sections of the media facilitated by con-temporary technology. It is not just an economic process, how-ever, and is evident across all facets of society. The responses to this complex set of processes from a cultural and ethnic per-spective are equally varied and multi-faceted.

Perspectives and responses

It might be useful to examine a number of perspectives on this issue. Neo-liberal perspectives see globalization as a largely positive process with the emergence of increasingly unified global markets and the decline in centralized government con-trol over economic movement (McGrew 2000: 349), a somewhat dated view following the economic collapse of 2008. It is part of the natural progression of capitalism linked into technological development and facilitated by multinationals such as exploration companies like Exxon and BP and technologists like IBM, Apple and Microsoft. Neo-liberalists view most outcomes of globalization as positive. They counter the suggestion that globalization is making local cultures more homogeneous through a variety of conservative market-led arguments. Writers such as Appadurai, not necessarily a neo-liberal himself but someone whose arguments have been adopted by neo-liberals, suggest that in this (supposed) post post-colonial world there is much to celebrate in the transformation and adoption of cultural flows (Appadurai 1999: 220). This involves the convergence and divergence of a series of grouped phenomena, including media, finance, technology and so on, that have replaced old-style colonialism and constitute a form of positive globalism. Appadurai sees globalization as consisting of a series of new emergent 'scapes', such as mediascapes and technoscapes, which can sit comfortably alongside the traditional cultural landscapes of art, countryside, heritage and media. This movement of people and ideas, manifested in refugee or diasporic communities, for example, also plays a part in the expansion of diversity and develops proponents and advocates of these evolving scapes.

Through the adoption of this argument one can suggest that in addition globalization has lead to cultural diversity and autonomy. It has given a new media voice to the subaltern. The transmission of local or individual movements on a global basis through the Internet has opened up a global audience to previous silent voices. It is argued that the adoption and appreciation of indigenous peoples, their dress, music and lifeways, could not have been propagated without this opening up of the world cultural domain. Knowledge of these peoples may previously have been open only to anthropologists or colonial governments, but now their clothing, goods and ethical products are freely available in the high street. Similarly, the supporters of indigenous causes such as the 'peasant' movements of South America have their own access to media, and political policies directed towards them may not now be solely dictated by self-serving colonial or dictatorial powers.

An alternative or radical perspective sees globalization as a largely negative phenomenon and as a form of neo-imperialism. The G7 states, using agencies such as the World Bank, the IMF and various trade agreements, all linked to multinational corporations, are primary drivers behind the developments leading to increased economic differentiation and marginalization of countries in the South (McGrew 2000: 350). One of the issues here is that 'Northern' interests and agencies largely lead development and the globalization process. Hence there is the potential for the imposition of external or often alien values and the breaking up of collective national identity (Allen & Eade 2000). This is one of the key aspects of power relationships in the development process. Contradictions in inherent societal values, for example, can lead to misunderstanding, disagreement or even conflict. If most development is led by the North then it is Northern cultural values and norms that effectively lead development. Cultural homogeneity is then seen as an inevitable consequence of these processes. Cultural uniformity is also represented in the increasing sameness of dress across Africa and the general abandonment of traditional dress. This was initially encouraged by Western missionary activity but now has become a form of aid in itself through the discarding of unsold or outdated Western clothes through various agencies. Thus we witness the proliferation of Western dress styles across Southern countries as a result of the redistribution of old clothing stock from established retail institutions. There is perhaps a certain irony here, given that many of the ranges would originally have been manufactured in developing countries.

Globalization is seen as eroding cultural authenticity, with the emergence, for example, of uniform high streets, outlets and diffusion of Western franchises, often referred to as McDonaldization. The commodification of culture is also an issue with the potential to exploit indigenous communities. The expansion of global tourism is an exemplar of this process.

3. Issues and threats

The removal of tribal groupings from the Masai plateau to facilitate tourism and the exclusion of local communities from visitor participation at World Heritage Sites represent elements of this issue. We then see the commodification of landscape for external persons and the creation of hierarchical power relations between North and South, visitor and indigenous, rich and poor. The erection of hotels and visitor facilities by waterfronts, in historic urban areas or adjacent to important heritage sites can create resentment and societal division. There are, of course, two sides to this argument. Tourism is an industry and can lead to opportunity. However, more often than not in many of the African countries tourism benefits few and affects many. Again tourism is only one facet of globalization. The emergence and creation of new markets can lead to industrialization, development and the exploitation of resources. Unfortunately, in an African context, much of this development has occurred in a largely unregulated manner at the expense of environment and living space.

A third, and increasingly recognized perspective, is that of the Transformationalists, where political power is being reconfigured allowing non-state powers into the equation and the emergence of power units in the South and transboundary solidarity (McGrew 2000, 353). Poverty is also viewed as a global phenomenon with new patterns of exclusion evident in the North and South. Globalization, then, is largely a product of modernity and the various forces and agencies that emerge within this process. A complex set of cultural responses to this can be discerned. Cultural protectionism can emerge as one response to the perceived impact of homogeneity. France and Canada, for example, have both introduced policies to protect their respective state film industries through subsidies and quotas (Palmer 2004). Indeed, the emergence of Bollywood as a direct challenger to Hollywood is evidence of the cultural power and differing values emerging in new North/South relationships. The first two perspectives above have constructed polar arguments about cultural responses to globalization. Yet it is such an enormous arena that there simply cannot be just two

59

responses. Instead multi-vocality is one of the key components of the transformationalist argument.

Ultimately, three perceived generalized responses to globalization can be identified within the sphere of culture and ethnicity. The first, largely negative, response sees globalization leading to cultural convergence, increasing the uniformity of lifeways and leading to the breakdown of many traditional norms and values within society. Extreme responses can also be seen through the isolation or encouragement of particular societies or groups, encouraging new nationalism and forms of racism. An opposite argument suggests that globalization has led in some circumstances to cultural empowerment and a renewed and strengthened sense of identity. This, of course, is a linked argument that can lead to a variety of responses. In this argument globalization is seen as acting as an agent of diversity and multi-culturalism. A third perspective would see cultural reaction to globalization as representing a combination of the previous two responses. Globalization is such a complex and diverse process that we can and should not see singular responses to the process. A recognition of the value and importance of these processes needs then to be integrated into the developmental process which can no longer be simply economic but instead is integrative of social and cultural factors. This can in essence help in providing a voice and inclusive role to the beneficiaries of international development.

4

Cultural resource management in Africa

The beginnings of contemporary archaeology in Africa can be traced back to Napoleon's invasion of Egypt (1798-1801) which involved numerous expeditions to survey and catalogue that country's built and material cultural heritage. In the nineteenth century, when European antiquarian activity was largely concentrated in North Africa, a significant quantity of cultural artefacts and pieces of art were plundered from their country of origin and deposited in the major world museums of the time. A number of European officials based in various countries began to develop an exclusive research tradition situated within a Western historical tradition with little regard for developing local institutions or expertise to take ownership of their regional material and built cultural heritage. Ernest-Théodore Hamy in West Africa published a number of ethnographic papers between 1877 and 1907, while Maurice Delafosse, French governor-general of the West African colonies, engaged in studies of past 'civilization' while enforcing colonial policies (Holl 1995: 190). In Northern Africa scientific archaeology emerges during the 1880s with the work of Flinders Petrie and later George Reisner (Horton 2008: 95). Early investigations across Eastern Africa included the Aksum Expedition of 1906 and the various investigations carried out at Great Zimbabwe from the 1880s through to the first decades of the twentieth century.

During the colonial period following the end of World War I and up to independence, a series of museums and cultural institutions were established across Africa. These were largely set up and staffed by European civil servants who had developed an appreciation of a particular country's heritage. Museums were founded in modern Ghana and Nigeria and the Institut Français d'Afrique Noire (IFAN) was formed. The establishment of such centres is reflective of broader colonial practice where the colonizer establishes Westernist cultural programmes of interpretation and curation. Many of these programmes, especially those involving survey and exploration, suited the colonial regime in terms of mapping territory and furthering understanding of resource availability and population make up. There were few, if any, local voices involved in these initiatives. To what extent these early archaeologists were complicit in the maintenance of colonialism or were simply products of their time is debatable. Whatever the case, they established the basis of the subsequent heritage institutions and bodies that emerged in many post-independent countries.

The first Pan-African Congress of Prehistory was held in 1947 at Nairobi under the guidance of Louis Leakey; a second congress was held in Algiers in 1952. Leakey had been working for decades investigating Stone Age sites and had generated global interest in his findings. Archaeology departments were established soon afterwards in a number of countries, building on existing units in various South African universities. With independence growth continued to a certain extent with the creation of government departments and national museums charged with the protection of their county's cultural resources. Unfortunately funding has not matched this pace of development, with many of these institutions continuing to struggle and compete for limited finances.

Legislation

As in most countries around the world, legislation has been one of the primary tools used in heritage management in Africa. While much of newly independent Francophile North and West Africa inherited relatively uniform legislation following a 1955 colonies decree, the majority of the former British colonies did not. In these countries legislation varied and was dependent on the particular level of colonial engagement with the area. The former Portuguese colonies did not inherit heritage legislation. In recent years a number of countries have updated their relevant statutes to take account of contemporary concerns and changing national values. The extent to which these acts have been successful is, however, varied. The key to the successful enactment of any environmental legislative programme is enforcement and unfortunately few African countries have the resources to ensure a full record of compliance. Poor governance and corruption play their part, while well funded external agents such as developers and antiquity dealers find it relatively easy to circumvent local controls. Increased resources for implementation are a necessary product of any interventionist strategy, but equally the international global governance community has its role to play in ensuring tighter controls on the antiquities trade, corporate transparency for many multinational companies and institutions and a global sense of responsibility towards heritage protection. Ultimately while a number of countries have strong controls and protection on paper a large number of others have little if any structures in place to safeguard heritage. This is an issue that needs to be addressed.

The countries with relevant legislation tend to take a broadly similar approach. Each attempts to define the type of cultural heritage present in their country and outline a number of ways in which that heritage can be protected. There tends to be a hierarchical approach towards protection, with most countries choosing to designate a small number of sites as national monuments and concentrate most protection efforts on these with little mention of cultural landscape approaches. A sample of legislation is presented here to provide a taster of the type of control in place across the continent. In North Africa Algeria's Excavation and Protection of Historic Monuments and Sites Ordinance no. 67-281, 1967, puts all cultural property in state ownership and outlaws its destruction. Monuments are defined as movable and immovable and include marine sites and finds.

In Libya, under the Antiquities, Archaeological Sites and Monuments Law no. 11, 1953, all antiquities over 100 years old and anthropological, animal or botanical remains predating AD 600 ultimately belong to the state and are registered on an inventory. Egypt's Protection of Antiquities Law no. 215 (revised no. 529, 1953 and no. 24, 1965) gives a degree of protection to known movable and immovable monuments and antiquities that belong to the State.

Ethiopia's Proclamation no. 229, 1966, defines an antiquity as any product of human historical endeavour and the government can confiscate any antiquity for its collection, while in Rwanda cultural property, including sites and objects, are protected by the state and registered on an inventory under Ordinance 22/112, 1956. In Tanzania the Antiquities Act of 1964 (amended in 1979) is the primary legislative tool for the protection of the archaeological resource. The resource is defined as any relic or object produced before 1863 and any human, faunal or fossil **remains**, and any painting, carving or monument. All cultural property belongs ultimately to the state and can be registered on an inventory. While there is no specific provision for submerged heritage, emergency provisions are available to the ministry with responsibility for cultural heritage to designate anything of national importance. While Zanzibar is part of the Tanzanian union, cultural heritage is dealt with separately. Its original Antiquities Act dates to 1927 and was later amended a number of times including 1984 and 2002. Under this act all heritage has the potential to be protected with the relevant minister able to declare anything an historical site and with the powers to bring land under governmental control. In 2006 a further amendment was added that had provision for underwater heritage following the activities of treasure hunters operating on a 'for profit' basis.

In Nigeria the Antiquities Ordinance of 1953 and Antiquities Regulations, 1957, were enacted following an initial 1924 ordinance controlling the export of art items (Shyllon 1996: 236). Material culture and sites made before 1918 ultimately belong to the state and are listed on an inventory and protected from destruction. Under Ghana's National Museum Decree, 1969, and National Museum Regulations, 1969, an antiquity is defined as an object of archaeological interest made before 1900. All known antiquities are protected from alienation and the state can declare national monuments and include them on an inventory. The Public Records Act, 1967 (amended 1969) in Gambia states that historical matter of any kind, nature and description can be transferred to or acquired by the Public Record Office.

South Africa probably has the most comprehensive and enforceable legislation of any of the African countries. The National Heritage Resources Act no. 25 of 1999 created a series of heritage organizations and initiatives aimed at safeguarding the nation's cultural heritage. As well as establishing a national heritage agency, the Act allowed for the designation of national and provincial heritage sites, with the sites being marked by plaques of similar signage. A series of heritage registers were to be incorporated into any urban or rural spatial planning scheme, structures older than 60 years old required a demolition permit, while graves and burial places (including those of people involved in the liberation struggle) were to be automatically protected. The Act also allows for the designation of heritage areas to protect places of cultural and environmental interest, and the gazetteer of heritage objects was to be further enhanced in order to control their trade and export. Importantly the 1999 Act also recognizes archaeology as an environmental resource; developers must take due note of and assess any heritage remains before starting work. The principle of 'developer pays' is also contained within the text. Fines, equipment confiscation and community service are among the consequences of infringing the legislation, while communities are encouraged to become involved with their heritage through a grant scheme.

The principle of 'developer pays' also exists in Botswana (MacEarchern 2001) where the Monuments and Relics Act of 1970 'provides for the better preservation and protection of ancient monuments, ancient workings, relics and other of aesthetic, archaeological, historical or scientific value or interest'. Ancient monuments are defined as 'any building or ruin, stone circle, grave, cave, rock shelter, midden, shell mound or other site or thing of a similar kind, which is known or believed to have been erected, constructed or used before 1st June, 1902'. In Malawi the 1965 Monuments Act 'makes provision for the preservation and protection of places of distinctive natural beauty and of sites, buildings and objects of archaeological, historical or of other interest'. This piece of legislation is centred around helping landowners to protect and preserve sites and providing advisory mechanisms for the location, preservation and protection of monuments and artefacts. Under Lesotho's Historical Monuments, Relics and Fauna and Flora Act no. 41, 1967, monuments are defined as areas of land with objects of archaeological/historical interest and include built monuments and areas or sites of historical or traditional importance. Relics include drawings and paintings executed by aboriginal peoples. Antiques are movable objects of importance over 100 years old and protected properties listed on an inventory. Angola's Ministerial Decree no. 6, 8 September 1938, followed by Legislative Act no. 2059, 16 June 1948, gives a degree of protection to monuments and objects of historical value. Finally, in Zimbabwe its colonial period Monuments and Relics Act, 1936, defines ancient monuments as any building, structure or ruin used by 'bushmen or other aboriginal inhabitants' dating to before 1890. Designated national monuments are given state protection and may be listed on an inventory. As with all aspects of Zimbabwean society, this Act and its associated governance structures are now in disarray.

National agencies

The key organizations with responsibility for heritage protection and management across Africa are national government agencies established by legislation (Fig. 7). While some countries have vested such responsibilities in particular ministries, others have chosen to position such powers within a national

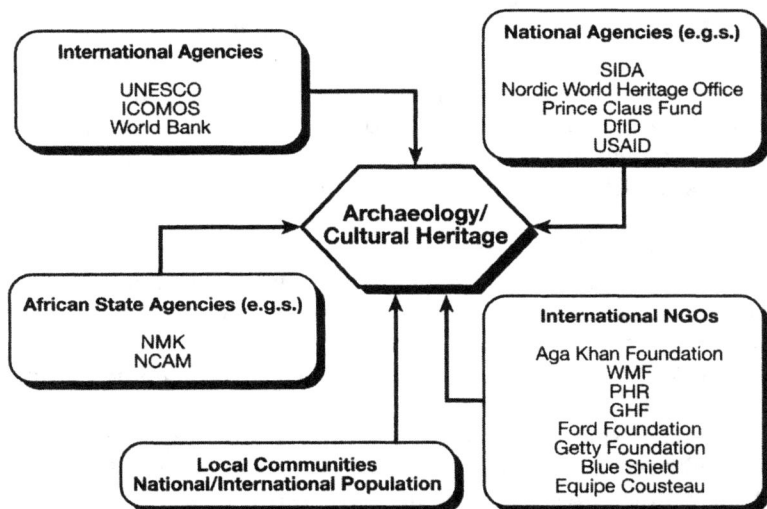

Fig. 7. National and international agencies involved with the
protection and management of archaeology and built
cultural heritage in Africa.

museum. The Supreme Council of Antiquities (SCA), Egypt, is
probably the best-known national agency in an African context
due to the extent of international research in that country and
the high profile of its Secretary General Dr Zahi Hawass. Its
origins lie in the nineteenth century when it served as an
antiquities service, but it gained its current format under
Presidential Decree no. 82 in 1994 as part of the Egyptian
Ministry of Culture. The SCA has a broad remit including the
regulation of archaeological activity in the country and the
conservation and protection of the country's heritage resources.
There are six subsections within the broader organization,
including the General Secretariat Sector, the Egyptian
(Pharaonic) and Graeco-Roman Antiquities Sector, the Coptic
and Islamic Antiquities Sector, the Antiquities and Museum
Financial Support Fund Sector, the General Projects Sector
and the Museums Sector. Also of relevance here is the Centre
for Documentation of Cultural and Natural Heritage, affiliated

with Bibliotheca Alexandrina and supported by the Ministry of Communications and Information Technology. The key remit of the centre is the documentation of Egyptian tangible and intangible cultural heritage and the digitization of heritage resources including the National Archives and the archives of El-Maktab El-Araby. It also has a training role in developing professional capacity in conservation and preservation.

The National Commission for Antiquities and Monuments (NCAM) in Sudan has an extremely active programme of internal research and engagement with the international archaeological community. It has administrative responsibility for the protection of monuments and licences the many foreign missions that work in the country.

Ghana's National Commission on Culture was established in 1990 'to manage from a holistic perspective, the cultural life of the country'. Its remit included the representation and preservation of traditions and cultural values and the promotion of a sense of unified and integrated national culture. The Ministry of Chieftaincy and Culture was subsequently established by the President in 1993 in order to 'preserve, conserve, develop, promote and present Ghanaian heritage institutions, arts, architecture, cultural sites and values to project the unique Ghanaian identity and national pride'. The Ghana Museums and Monuments Board (GMMB) is an integral part of the governance structure of the Ministry while affiliated organizations include the Institute of African Studies and the Department of Archaeology at the University of Ghana.

The National Commission for Museums and Monuments (NCMM) was established in 1977 in Nigeria to carry out the National Commission for Museums and Monuments Decree no. 77. One of the key components of this move was to tackle the illicit trade in artefacts. Unfortunately this trade continued and it appears that a number of museum staff were complicit in it (Brodie 2000). In 1999 the government established the Federal Ministry of Culture and Tourism of which NCMM is now a constituent part. The Commission's key roles include the management and preservation of national museums, antiquities and monuments throughout the country and the designation of sites as national monuments.

In Tanzania the Antiquities and Museum's Division of the Ministry of Natural Resources and Tourism has national responsibility for cultural heritage management. Its core objectives include the conservation, protection, research and development of the national cultural heritage, allowing that heritage sites constitute tourist attractions and centres for education for the population. Four hundred sites across mainland Tanzania have been protected and inventorized with *c.*120 being legally protected. The core functions of the organization make interesting reading and underlie their aspirational developmental and sustainable approach to cultural heritage in Tanzania. The organization's functions include the management of sites, giving due cognizance to associated cultural values; developing sustainable programmes of recording and research at sites on a regional and international level; developing sites as centres for education and tourism; and integrating community into the management and protection of these sites.

In South Africa the South African Heritage Resources Agency (SAHRA) is a statutory organization established under the National Heritage Resources Act as the national administrative body responsible for the protection of South Africa's cultural heritage. Its core objectives are 'to coordinate the identification and management of the national estate' (including sites, monuments, objects, places, graves, documents, art and music) and manage the system for the identification, assessment and management of heritage resources. Significantly a national resources survey was also established in 1999 in order to identify, locate and survey sites, monuments and objects of cultural significance. The establishment of an 'Inventory of the National Estate' represented an important step forward. The inventory is a database incorporating the following elements:

- all places and objects protected through the publication of notices in the Gazette or Provincial Gazette, whether in terms of the National Heritage Resources Act or provincial legislation;
- places and objects subject to general protections in terms of the Act or provincial legislation for the management of heritage resources;
- any other place and object considered to be of heritage significance; and all places and objects protected prior to 1999.

A series of common problems exist within the majority of these institutions, agencies and ministries across Africa. Most are severely underfunded, with limited resources. Few are engaged in comprehensive inventory activity as a consequence with many states maintaining gazetteers of a few hundred sites at the most. The finance and personnel is simply not available to allow for the comprehensive survey of their countries. This problem is further compounded by an over-emphasis on World Heritage Sites (Breen 2007) and a paucity of experience in dealing with and enforcing environmental impact assessment. Many of the agencies are also over-reliant on foreign academics and researchers to provide opportunities for training and research in their own countries. As a result much of the material that is recorded within the inventories is either based upon work carried out by former colonial officials or largely upon Western-led research agendas. The same problems apply to any training or education provided by foreign academics and agencies. This has lead in the most part to heritage inventories concentrating largely upon either rural prehistoric remains with an emphasis upon lithic and ceramic analyses or large monumental representations of high social status.

Research has begun to concentrate upon the more recent past in places like South Africa (examples are given elsewhere in this volume) and in so doing have engaged with social histories and historic memory. In this way, archaeology has become to some the study of the process of interaction between peoples regardless of period or temporal delineation. By using the archaeological tools of material analyses in regard to more recent events, those not represented in the traditional historic record can be given voice and form, making them active participants within our understanding of the past.

The development of what is known as 'post-medieval' or 'historical archaeology' has a strong relationship with the growth of archaeological practice in Africa outside European traditional elites. With the earlier colonial archaeologists investigating largely evolutionary development or Later Stone Age technologies, it fell to post-independence archaeologists to scrutinize cultural relationships from a material perspective, be this in the form of either ethno-archaeological research (Feierman 2002) or the examination of the development of identities (Chami 2006; Kusimba 1999). This research trajectory was a direct result of the circumstances under which archaeologists found themselves working. As the teaching of the subject increased (see below, section on 'Universities and research institutions'), students often underwent a combination of archaeological and historical training with the option of specializing in archaeology in their final undergraduate year. As a result of this disciplinary approach research into the relationships of power between indigenous and non-indigenous peoples have entered the archaeological debate and created a new generation of politicized archaeologists (see, for example, the work by Martin Hall and Nick Shepherd at the University of Cape Town), as well as stretching the more traditional approaches within non-European environments (see, for example, the ceramic analyses of Antonia Malan and Jane Klose, again at the University of Cape Town).

This blurring of traditional academic boundaries also raises a key issue of paper archive and library resource management. As archaeologists we now find ourselves delving more into collections of the written and cartographic record and as such must take responsibility for their safeguard and management just as much as for the archaeological environment. However, as will be discussed below in relation to museums, archives within Africa receive little if any government consideration and like the archaeological resource have been overlooked as a resource that could develop in an economically and culturally beneficial way. The documentary heritage resource can also be used developmentally and could play a key role in Africa as both an information source when militating against damage to the material heritage resource, as well as a tool in the negotiation of personal and national identities. In line with this, UNESCO established the *Memory of the World* Programme in 1992 which aimed not only to highlight the degenerating nature of many archives throughout the world but also to publicize the holdings of collections for the benefit and preservation of the world's documentary heritage as a whole. With this in mind the *Memory of the World Register* was founded in 1995 and through the website portal a number of national archives and pan-national archive research projects can be accessed, for example the Slave Trade Archives Project set up by UNESCO in 1999 and funded by the Norwegian Agency for Development Cooperation (NORAD). Further to this, the AAU has also developed the Database of African Theses and Dissertations, an ongoing programme designed to aid the dissemination of research through electronic and paper mediums. INASP has created the PERii initiative that aims to strengthen global research communication by delivering access to scholarly literature and publication in developing states. The Association of Commonwealth Universities (ACU) has devised the 'Protecting the African Library Scheme' to help universalities in Commonwealth developing countries secure access the scholarly literature.

Museums

Museums are complex institutions in Africa. Many were originally established as hobbyist centres by European settlers or colonial administrators. Many were used effectively to subjugate the indigenous populations through propagating the myth of backward, traditional and static societies that had changed little since the Stone Age. Most were removed both in a physical and theoretical sense from their national populations in so far as they became centres for externally led research, were perceived as elitist centres of knowledge and functioned primarily to service the tourist industry. Following independence many museums fell by the wayside and were seen as expensive bourgeois commodities that had little to offer national development or liberation strategies. A number of museums, however, were incorporated into the new regimes and used to promote ideals of a common past and a sense of national pride and identity. It was also recognized that museums have the potential to contribute strongly to the economy, to become centres for learning and education, to be the focus for community development and engagement, and to develop a sense of belonging and place. Unfortunately the sector remains maligned with Schmidt and McIntosh (1996: 7) arguing that museums are not working in Africa and are seen as removed, remote institutions that serve as shrines to government and fulfil largely tourist functions. Considerable problems also remain with the actual operation of the institutions. Many museum buildings are in a poor physical state, their collections remain undocumented and in poor storage conditions and there is limited professional capacity to run and further develop the sites. Tied to this is the static nature of many of their displays and exhibits which rarely change and do not encourage repeat visits. Museums are also low on government agendas when it comes to spreading finance and developing infrastructure. A number of museums have had particularly difficult histories. In 1965 it is alleged that Ethiopian UN forces looted the Elisabethville Museum in the Congo (LaGamma 1996: 94). The museum in the Somali capital was extensively looted and essentially destroyed following the outbreak of civil war across the country (Brandt & Mohamed 1996). When the Institut des Sciences Humaines in Cameroon was closed in the 1980s, artefacts were taken from its collections and used to fill holes in the street (MacEarchern 2001). There are a number of initiatives and organizations including ICOM, AFRI-COM and CHDA working to develop capacity in this area, and these will be addressed in later chapters.

There are hundreds of museums across the African continent. Suffice to say there is not room to deal with them individually here, but a number of notable sites warrant mention. The National Museums of Kenya (NMK) is one of the most progressive institutions in Africa. Originally a small colonial-period museum in Nairobi, it is now a large multidisciplinary institution established by an Act of Parliament, the Museums and Heritage Act 2006, 'whose role is to collect, preserve, study, document and present Kenya's past and present cultural and natural heritage'. It further defines its purpose as enhancing knowledge, appreciation, respect and sustainable utilization of these resources for the benefit of Kenya and the world. With a central base in Nairobi it operates a series of smaller museums and research centres across the country, including Lamu and Fort Jesus in Mombasa, as well as having responsibility for sites and monuments and a number of research bodies including the Institute of Primate Research. Importantly, following the passing of the Museums and Heritage Act 2006, the NMK is now effectively responsible for heritage management across the state. NMK's role has developed beyond the cultural sector and it has increasingly seen itself as promoting a sense of nationhood in Kenya across a number of different sociopolitical spheres.

The Egyptian Museum in Cairo was established by the government in 1835. It is one of the most venerable museums in Africa and houses an impressive collection of artefactual material. It moved to its current neo-classical building in 1900 and has become a centrepiece of the Egyptian tourist industry.

The National Museum of Botswana was established by an Act of Parliament in 1967 and subsequently came under government control in 1976. It functions primarily as an educational and research institution dedicated to understanding the past peoples and varying ethnicities of the country and past environments. Five subdivisions constitute the overall structure of the museum, of which archaeology is the largest and has responsibility for all monuments and antiquities. The others include salvage/rescue, research and information, old buildings, and a lesser unit dealing with the recording and management of archaeological collections. Probably uniquely among African museum services, it has a mobile outreach unit that brings the museum to the people of the country.

In Ghana the National Museum in Accra was formally opened in March 1957 following the country's independence. It was designed to instil a sense of national pride and to further understandings of the country's historical development. It is currently the largest museum operated by the Ghana Museums and Monuments Board.

Criticisms remain about the remoteness of many African museums from their people, but this is changing. A number of important initiatives over the past years have seen a shift away from traditionalist museums serving as monuments to the dead towards places celebrating the present. Robben Island in South Africa is one such example. Nelson Mandela spent much of his life incarcerated in this institution, and following the ascent of the ANC to power the new post-Apartheid regime established the former prison and leper colony as a monument to their leader and the liberation struggle (Shackley 2001). This was a contested process with some arguing that it did not give enough credence to others involved in the struggle such as the Pan African Congress. Some of these oversights have been rectified, with most agreeing that Robben Island 'should not be a shrine to suffering and hardship but to the "triumph of the human spirit over suffering and hardship" ' (Coombes 2003: 58). The District Six Museum is probably most representative of change and the re-engagement of people and communities with their past and heritage. Established in 1994, it celebrates the Cape Town district before it became a white area two decades earlier. Its exhibits and low technology displays allow people to reconnect and develop memories of the area. The success of this project has lead to other similar initiatives including those at Protea and Lwandle, while community-based projects are also developing in parts of East and West Africa (Hughes 2007).

Universities and research institutions

Universities play a key role in the heritage sector. They provide training and educational programmes to ensure a sufficient cohort of qualified people in the field as well as supplying opportunities for up-skilling and continuous professional development. These institutions also serve as centres for research and development and create programmes that further knowledge and understanding. Consequently a dynamic and properly funded university and third/fourth-level sector is crucial for both the social and economic development of any state. This is of course one of the fundamental problems experienced by various countries across the continent. There are many good universities present but they are, for the most part, underfunded and under-resourced. Issues such as access, the continuing brain drain and the upsurge of a plethora of private and largely unvalidated institutions pose serious threats to the sustainability of the third-level sector across Africa. The creation of archaeological research institutions and teaching programmes may also appear to be a low priority for many governments. Such programmes have often been seen as a luxury when there are more pressing concerns for the development of capacity in the educational, medical and economic spheres. There is a degree of validity in this prioritization, but archaeology and conservation research can have a proactive role to play in any modern state, as we have seen throughout this volume. Schmidt (1996) in an important account of the development of an archaeology unit in the University of Dar es Salaam during Tanzania's 'Socialist Era', writes of the opposition to such a venture from established academics who perceived it as a bourgeois occupation and who questioned whether archaeology would put food on the table. A unit was subsequently established and continues to function as one of the most progressive teaching and research centres across the region, making significant contributions to the subject and to society over the past twenty-five years. Interestingly, in the context of this study, it has also led to the establishment of a number of major research programmes across the sub-Saharan region funded by the Swedish international development agency. This will be examined in greater depth in later chapters.

Somewhat unsurprisingly, given the wealth of archaeological material in this region, North Africa has a number of well-established departments. A vibrant Faculty of Archaeology has been present at the University of Cairo for many years. It teaches a broad range of courses in Egyptian and Islamic archaeology as well as conservation practice. It continues to be both a research hub and a central training ground for many of the region's archaeologists. Archaeology is also present at the University of Alexandria, which recently inaugurated the Alexandria Centre for Maritime Archaeology and Underwater Cultural Heritage, a major research centre funded by the EU TEMPUS programme. In 1964 the Department of Archaeology was established at the University of Khartoum. Initially it offered only postgraduate training, including a Higher Diploma in Egyptology, but it has subsequently developed to offer a full spectrum of undergraduate and postgraduate courses. It is also an active research department with projects ongoing throughout northern Sudan.

Archaeology departments were established in 1963 at Legon, Ghana and Nsukka, Nigeria, while a third centre was established at Ibadan, Nigeria (Schmidt 1995: 128). Thurstan Shaw was granted a research professorship in archaeology at Ibadan in 1963 at the Institute of African Studies, followed by the formal establishment of a full department in 1970/71. Professor Bassey Andah led the movement towards a change in the 1980s when the department became Archaeology and Anthropology in an attempt to increase student numbers. In 1981 a second department was set up at the University of Nigeria, Nsukka and a third established at Ahmadu Bello University Zaria in 2006. The Nsukka department is now known as Archaeology and Tourism in an attempt to make it more relevant and improve student numbers. Curricula at these universities are traditional and centred around discovery, recovery, documentation and interpretation and the material culture of sites at Ife, Benin, Nok and Igbo (Gundun 2008: 1). These programmes suffer from significant under-funding, with little emphasis being placed on theoretical and technological advances in the subject. Laboratory provision is virtually non-existent and students have only limited exposure to the applications of IT to archaeology. By the early 1980s archaeology was also being developed at universities in Benin, Togo and Burkina Faso, but these initiatives suffered with the major problems affecting the region by the middle of the decade (Posnansky 1996).

South Africa is relatively provided with university centres of teaching and research. Archaeology departments exist at the University of South Africa, with its Department of Anthropology and Archaeology, and at the University of Witwatersrand with its School of Geography, Archaeology and Environmental Science. The Department of Archaeology at the University of Cape Town enjoys an international reputation and has research interests in evolution, the archaeology and anthropology of modern humans, and early hunter-gatherer, pastoralist and farming communities across southern Africa. The department also has a strong historical archaeology programme and specialises in archaeometric and materials research. Cultural resource management is an emerging aspect of its programmes. Other countries with notably strong and progressive centres include the aforementioned archaeology unit at the University of Dar es Salaam, Tanzania, and the archaeology unit at the University of Botswana.

Within South and West Africa two regional research management associations also exist, designed specifically to foster partnerships between researchers and research institutions. The South African Research and Innovation Management Association (SARIMA) and the West African Research and Innovation Management Association (WARIMA). Although not specifically aimed at archaeologists, their objectives are:

- professional development and capacity building;
- promotion of best practice;
- increasing awareness of research and innovation in academic and public fora;

- advocacy of appropriate national and institutional policy in support of research and innovation;
- advancement of science, technology and innovation, including addressing the asymmetries in access to, and diffusion of, knowledge between 'North' and 'South';
- advancement of a code of professional standards;
- enhancement of the profile of the profession (www.warima.org 2009, www.sarima.co.za 2009).

These two associations demonstrate an awareness of the need to develop cross-border research management structures within which archaeological researchers can benefit from knowledge sharing with those from outside their particular field, as well as through identifying funding opportunities fostered through partnership. In this same way, the Association of African Universities (AAU) aims to promote collaboration between teaching and research institutions, and importantly community engagement. The AAU headquarters is in Accra, Ghana. It was created at a meeting in Morocco in 1967 following a conference organized by UNESCO. The Association now has some 199 members drawn from universities all across the African continent.

Finally, a series of research institutions funded by various external states and bodies are also an integral part of the academic and research landscape. The British Institute of History and Archaeology in Eastern Africa was founded in 1960 in Dar es Salaam before moving to Nairobi where it is now known as the British Institute in Eastern Africa. Its original aim was to facilitate research across Tanzania, Kenya and Uganda, and it now promotes research into the archaeology, history, linguistics and anthropology of Eastern Africa as a whole. Other state-sponsored organizations located in Africa include the French Institute for Research in Africa (IFRA) and the French Institute in South Africa (IFSA).

5

An agency and legislative framework

Following the end of the Second World War there was an increased awareness of the hugely destructive nature of war and its catastrophic effect on the culture and built heritage of the world's populations. A series of initiatives was undertaken to mitigate the future consequences of conflict upon cultural resources, resulting in the establishment of a number of international agencies tasked with the protection and promotion of cultural awareness and understanding. This also constituted recognition of the global nature of heritage and its central role in developing a sense of belonging and of place. This chapter examines the role and function of organizations at three different levels – international multilateral organizations, national agencies and institutions, and non-governmental organizations (NGOs). A brief examination will also be conducted of the legislative framework deployed across this area. It will quickly become apparent that there are a multitude of players in the heritage sphere, drawn from across the public and private sectors. While it is encouraging that this level of input exists, the sector is not without its faults and has seen its fair share of failures. An analysis of this complexity will be dealt with in later chapters.

International organizations

The United Nations

Following the end of the First World War in 1919, the Treaty of Versailles established the League of Nations 'to promote international cooperation and to achieve peace and security'. This organization could be viewed as a precursor of the United Nations, which came into being on 24 October 1945. The essence of the organization was the UN Charter, which set out a series of principles and findings designed to create a better, more secure world, centred on human rights and global security. Four primary purposes are laid out in Chapter 1 of the charter; they include the need to maintain international peace and security, to develop peaceful international relations, to approach global socio-economic and humanitarian problems on an international co-operative basis, and to be the central player and conduit for the above actions. Since that time the UN has developed into an extremely complex entity with a myriad of internal divisions and over 30 affiliated organizations that make up the UN System. Within the UN there are five primary units based at its headquarters in New York: the General Assembly, the Security Council, the Economic and Social Council, the Trusteeship Council, and the Secretariat. A sixth unit, the International Court of Justice, is located at The Hague. A series of other organizations or 'specialized agencies' are affiliated to the UN, including the International Monetary Fund, the World Bank and the World Health Organization. UNESCO, or the United Nations Educational, Scientific and Cultural Organization, is one of these specialized autonomous agencies and is of most relevance to this study.

UNESCO

UNESCO was formed on 16 November 1945 to promote 'education for all, cultural development, protection of the world's natural and cultural heritage, international cooperation in science, press freedom and communication' (Fig. 8). By 2008 there were 193 member states and six associate members within the organization. Aruba, the British Virgin Islands and the Cayman Islands are among the associate member states. 182 member states have permanent delegations at UNESCO while 195 national commissions have been set up by member states to

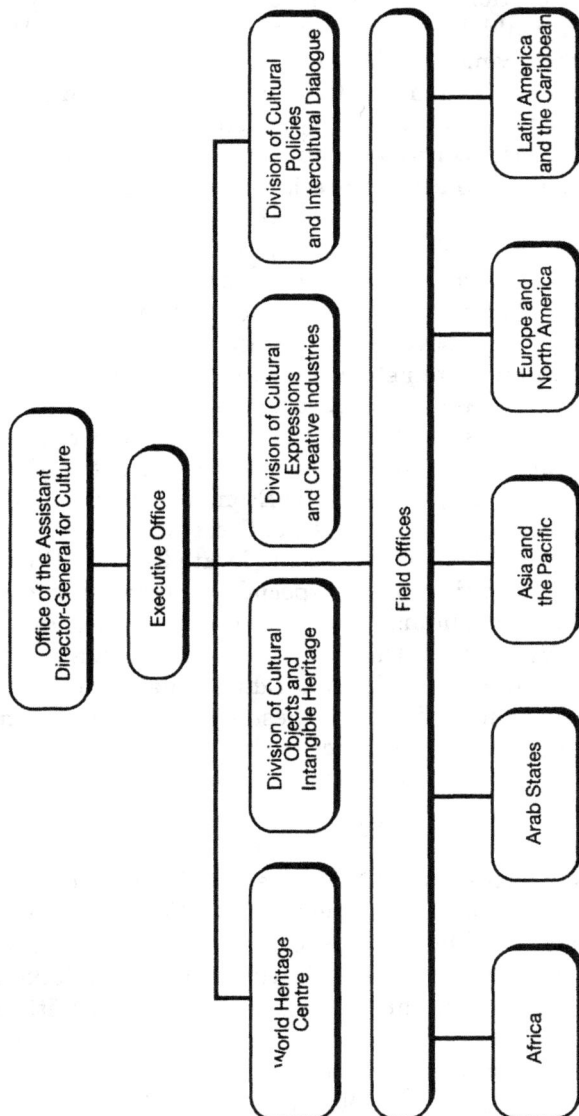

Fig. 8. Chart demonstrating the organization structure of UNESCO.

facilitate operations and interchange with UNESCO. In addition, the organization has working relations with a large number of inter-governmental organizations (IGOs) and other institutions like the European Commission and multilateral development banks. Finally, UNESCO lays particular emphasis on working with civil society and maintains relations with NGOs and other relevant organizations while also encouraging sustainable relationships with the private sector. UNESCO works within six specific thematic areas: Education, Natural Sciences, Social and Human Sciences, Culture, Communication and Information and Special Themes. While these are all cross-cutting areas, it is the theme of culture that has most bearing here. Within this theme there are eight further sub-themes including Cultural Diversity, World Heritage, Intangible Heritage, Movable Heritage and Museums, Creativity, Dialogue, Normative Action and Emergency Situations. An integral part of UNESCO's work is the promotion and protection of cultural resources and to this end it has developed a number of conventions to support its role.

Convention	Year
Universal Copyright Convention	1952, 1971
Protection of Cultural Property in the Event of Armed Conflict	1954
Prohibiting and Preventing the Illicit Import, Export and Transfer of Cultural Property	1970
Protection of the World Cultural and Natural Heritage	1972
Protection of the Underwater Cultural Heritage	2001
Safeguarding of the Intangible Cultural Heritage	2003
Protection and Promotion of the Diversity of Cultural Expressions	2005

Table 5.1. UNESCO conventions on the promotion and protection of cultural heritage.

UNESCO's current 2008/09 Major Programme IV (Culture) will pursue the 'Promotion of cultural diversity and dialogue among peoples' and will take the intersectoral lead for contributing to the three related strategic objectives: 'Strengthening the contribution of culture to sustainable development', 'Demonstrating the importance of exchanges and dialogue among cultures for social cohesion, reconciliation and the establishment of a culture of peace'. and 'Protecting and enhancing cultural heritage in a sustainable manner'. Its specific targets (Document 34 C/5 Draft) under this programme include;

IV.1 Protecting and conserving immovable cultural and natural properties, in particular through the effective implementation of the World Heritage Convention.

IV.2 Safeguarding living heritage, particularly through the promotion and implementation of the Intangible Cultural Heritage Convention.

IV.3 Enhancing the protection of cultural objects, the fight against illicit trafficking in them, and the development of museums as places for access to knowledge.

IV.4 Protecting and promoting the diversity of cultural expressions through the implementation of the 2005 Convention and the development of cultural and creative industries.

IV.5 Promoting the understanding and development of intercultural dialogue and peace.

IV.6 Mainstreaming within national policies, the links between cultural diversity, intercultural dialogue and sustainable development.

A number of these objectives specifically mention Africa, in particular IV.4, which states as a targeted outcome the 'Better recognition of original and innovative initiatives to promote the cultural and creative industries, and the role of cultural events in regional integration strengthened, in particular in Africa'. Other targets that are applicable in an African context include the inclusion of more sites on the World Heritage list, an increase in capacity levels, increased involvement of communities in heritage, and the protection of cultural heritage during periods of conflict. The integration of cultural and built heritage into sustainable development frameworks is also strongly advocated.

ICOM

ICOM (the International Council of Museums) was established in 1946 as an international organization for the promotion and development of museums. It is a non-profit NGO that has established a formal association and advisory status with UNESCO. It functions in a number of ways including facilitating an international network for museum professionals and institutions as well as campaigning strongly against the illicit trade in cultural property. ICOM established a specific programme for Africa (AFRICOM) to facilitate the fight against this trade. It was also aimed at developing North/South collaboration, capacity building, education and awareness and research. It produced a series of important publications aimed at facilitating these initiatives, including a handbook on standards and documentation and one on looting in Africa including a list of 100 missing objects associated with this activity. In October 1999 AFRICOM became the International Council of African Museums, an autonomous pan-African organization for museums, based in Nairobi, Kenya.

ICMOS

The first Congress of Architects and Specialists of Historic Buildings held in Paris in 1957 recommended that the member states of UNESCO join the International Centre for the Study of the Preservation and Restoration of Cultural Property (IC-CROM) based in Rome. At its second congress in Rome seven years later it adopted a resolution submitted by UNESCO for the establishment of an International Council on Monuments and Sites (ICOMOS). The same conference embedded the principles of the organization in the 1964 International Charter on the Conservation and Restoration of Monuments and Sites (the Venice Charter). ICOMOS is now an international NGO with nearly 8,000 members. Its primary aim is to work for the conservation and protection of cultural heritage places, and it operates through an international multidisciplinary expert group dedicated to best practice and standards for all forms of built heritage. ICOMOS includes among its objectives the development of international networks and forums to disseminate information relating to conservation practice, to develop documentation centres, and to facilitate training and provision of expertise in this area. Specifically it encourages the development of national committees, defines standards and management techniques, advises UNESCO on its World Heritage list and organizes expert missions. ICOMOS also issues an annual or biannual heritage at risk report. Its 2006/07 report lists a number of sites under threat in Africa, including the Mtwapa Heritage Site and the Qorahey Wells in Kenya and the Mausoleum of Medracen in Algeria. Worryingly a number of rock art sites in the Western Sahara had been vandalized by UN soldiers and were listed as being under threat.

Blue Shield

The 1954 Hague Convention assigned the symbol of a blue shield to built heritage sites so that they would theoretically be protected from destruction during conflict and war. It was following the example of the International Red Cross in adopting an easily recognisable symbol to aid identification in conflict zones. In 1996 the International Committee of the Blue Shield (ICBS) was established and charged with working towards the protection of cultural heritage under threat from conflict and natural disasters. Three years later the Second Protocol to the Hague Convention, agreed in April 1999, gave the ICBS a new role, to advise the inter-governmental Committee for Protection of Cultural Property in the Event of Armed Conflict. Its heritage remit is wide and covers sites and monuments, archives, libraries and museums. Its defined mission is to 'work for the protection of the world's cultural heritage by coordinating preparations to meet and respond to emergency situations' (ICBS 2008). The ICBS is currently formed by five NGOs – the Co-ordinating Council of Audiovisual Archives Associations (CCAAA), the International Council on Archives (ICA), the International Council of Museums (ICOM), the International Council on Monuments and Sites (ICOMOS) and the International Federation of Library Associations and Institutions (IFLA). Its primary objectives can be summarized as facilitating international responses to threats or emergencies threatening cultural property and ensuring safeguards are in place in the event of risk elevation. The organization also engages in the training of experts to deal with disaster episodes and acts as an international advisory and consultative body.

The World Bank

The World Bank plays an increasingly important role in cultural heritage management across the Global South. It consists of two institutions, the International Bank for Reconstruction and Development (IBRD) and the International Development Association (IDA). It is not a conventional bank as such but is instead owned by 185 countries and provides financial assistance and support for developing nations. The IDA was established in 1960 to assist the world's poorest nations while the IBRD focuses on middle income and creditworthy countries. The Bank perceives cultural resources as finite, key assets for economic and social development and as constituting a central element for identity and cultural practice. It has developed objective OP/BP 4.11 on Physical Cultural Resources 'to avoid, or mitigate, adverse impacts on cultural resources from development projects that the World Bank finances' (World Bank 2006). This objective replaced the 1986 OPN 11.03, Management of Cultural Property in Bank-Financed Projects. Such impacts have to be considered at an early project stage and are dealt with through environmental assessment. Importantly, the Bank also recognizes that capacity building may need to run alongside such assessment in the context of its country assistance projects. It has financed a number of interventionist programmes in Africa over the past two decades and remains an important source of finance and development assistance. Of particular note have been its interventions as part of its investment in the MENA (Middle East and North Africa) region. Further details on this and other work is included in the following chapter.

International legislation and agreements

A series of important international conventions and agreements are relevant here. Fundamental to these is Article 22 of the Universal Declaration of Human Rights, adopted by the UN General Assembly in 1948, which states:

> Everyone, as a member of society, has the right to social security and is entitled to realization, through national effort and international co-operation and in accordance with the organization and resources of each State, of the economic, social and *cultural rights* indispensable for his dignity and the free development of his personality.

Further, the UN's International Covenant on Economic, Social and Cultural Rights which came into force in 1976 recognizes the right of everyone to '... take part in cultural life; and to enjoy the benefits of scientific progress and its applications ... while recognizing the benefits to be derived from the encouragement and development of international contacts and co-operation in the scientific and cultural fields'.

The Convention for the Protection of Cultural Property in the Event of Armed Conflict (1954), better known as the Hague Convention, and its two protocols (1954 and 1999) were developed specifically to lessen the effects of war on all forms of cultural heritage, including archaeology and built heritage, art, books and other objects. Each of the states that have signed the Convention undertakes to fulfil a number of obligations, including the protection of cultural property during national and international armed conflict as well as in times of peace. In preparation for such events they must put preventive mechanisms in place for protection, including the listing of sites and objects in the International Register of Cultural Property under Special Protection and the labelling of sites with special markers. Additionally, specialist units within the military are to be established with a specific brief to protect cultural heritage. Further protocols prohibit the export of cultural material from occupied territory and the appropriation of cultural property as war reparations.

In an attempt to counter the international trade in and theft of illicit artefacts UNESCO developed the Convention on the Means of Prohibiting and Preventing the Illicit Import, Export and Transfer of Ownership of Cultural Property (1970), an international, multilateral legal instrument. Cultural material, as defined in the Convention, includes products of archaeological excavations (including regular and clandestine) or of archaeological discoveries; elements of artistic or historical monuments or archaeological sites that have been dismembered; antiquities more than one hundred years old, such as inscriptions, coins and engraved seals; and objects of ethnological interest. As part of their responsibilities towards protection each country undertakes to develop an appropriate set of laws to protect their cultural heritage and prevent illegal export of material. They are also obliged to establish national inventories of movable and immovable cultural heritage and to develop suitable institutions for their preservation and display. All excavation should be regulated and a series of initiatives implemented surrounding the care, education and promotion of cultural heritage. By 2008 116 states were party to the Convention.

In further response to continued concerns about the illicit trade in cultural activity, the UNIDROIT Convention on Stolen or Illegally Exported Cultural Objects (1995) was formulated. UNIDROIT is the International Institute for the Unification of Private Law, an independent inter-governmental organization based in Rome that studies the requirements and methodologies 'for modernizing, harmonizing and coordinating private and in particular commercial law between States and groups of

States'. One of the Convention's primary purposes is to facilitate the restitution and return of cultural objects between states. Such material includes archaeological artefacts, art, music, books, architecture and a plethora of other defined items. The Convention is complementary to the 1970 UNESCO Convention but allows for the use of private law and defined owners to use the court system of particular countries to recover stolen cultural property. By 2004 23 states were party to this Convention.

Additional agreements of relevance include the Convention on the Protection of the Underwater Cultural Heritage (2001) adopted by UNESCO General Conference in that year. The Convention recognizes the importance of submerged cultural heritage and the threat posed to this material by commercial operations. It aims to limit the impacts of such activity and further develop capacity in relation to the management and protection of the resource, and it addresses material deposited outside territorial waters. Both the Convention for the Safeguarding of the Intangible Cultural Heritage (2003) and the Convention on the Protection and Promotion of the Diversity of Cultural Expressions (2005) develop further our awareness of the importance of intangible cultural heritage and the mechanisms required for developing protective measures and ensuring the sustainability of these resources. Of final note is the 1998 Stockholm Conference, a UNESCO Intergovernmental Conference on Cultural Policies for Development. The conference adopted an action plan that addressed the need for capacity building, and specifically the concept of cultural heritage being utilized in developing societal understandings and economic and tourist benefits.

National agencies

National or state-funded ministries or agencies are crucial components of the international development framework. It is these organizations that are responsible for the management and distribution of each country's international aid budget and for the policies and directions towards which this funding is aimed. There is no uniformity of approach between these institutions, with their activities being guided by the ideology and structure of their individual governments. Some have a regional orientation while others focus on particular spheres or issues. In terms of financial aid contributions as a percentage of GDP, it is the Scandinavian and north-west European countries that are most active. It is also apparent that a number of these countries regard cultural capacity building as an integral part of their agendas, an approach shared by few other nations. The Swedish International Development Cooperation Agency (SIDA) has been especially proactive in this arena. It is a government agency whose governing principle is the provision of 'international development cooperation' as opposed to hierarchical assistance. SIDA works in over twenty target countries but has supported projects in most Global South nations and across Eastern Europe on the basis that each country is responsible for its own development. It works primarily through a process of partnership within civic and public society to allow 'poor people to improve their living conditions'. Of particular note here is SIDA's support for cultural heritage projects in Africa, Latin America, the Middle East and Asia. These projects are primarily aimed at developing protection, management and research projects centred on the sustainable use of cultural heritage. Specifically, the agency supports conservation practice and research on built heritage and environment that is inclusive of community. It also supports archaeology programmes that allow subaltern groups and people with no written history to develop understandings of their past. SIDA also has an active museums support programme which aims to develop conservation capacity and generate accessibility and engagement of communities with their heritage. The Swedish-African Museum Programme (SAMP) also allows for the twinning of institutions, including the District Six Museum with Malmo Museums. Past partners in this wide range of SIDA work include universities, culture ministries, NGOs and regional networks.

The Norwegian Agency for Development Cooperation (NO-RAD), operating within the Norwegian Ministry of Foreign Affairs (MFA) initially became involved with supporting culture in the 1980s. It defines cultural heritage as 'the legacy of physical artifacts, buildings, sites and landscapes, and intangible products, customs and practices of a group or society that are inherited from past generations, maintained in the present and bestowed for the benefit of future generations'. Between 1997 and 2005 cultural heritage was supported by a strategy for environment in development cooperation before becoming integrated into a strategy for cultural cooperation that is scheduled to run until 2015. The funding of cultural activities is broadly based, with support being generated and channelled through the MFA, NORAD and individual embassies, while the Norwegian Directorate for Cultural Heritage, the Nordic World Heritage Foundation, the Ministry of Environment and the Ministry of Culture are also integrated into the process. The Norwegians adopt a rights-based agenda and see culture as important for development and poverty alleviation.

In the United States USAID is a federal agency that provides assistance to so-called developing countries. Its work is intrinsically linked to the furtherance of American foreign policy and supports work in the fields of economic growth, agriculture and trade, global health, democracy, conflict prevention and humanitarian assistance. It has a significant presence in Africa with a number of missions and regional centres. While USAID has been active in financing and engaging with heritage partnerships, supporting research and developing a series of capacity building ventures in North Africa, most of its recent work in this area has occurred in places like Iraq. Other national agencies have also engaged in this type of activity in Africa but to a lesser extent, including the Japan International Cooperation Agency (JICA) and the Japan Bank for International Cooperation (JBIC), both of which have funded cultural heritage projects. Worryingly, a large number of other national agencies have no involvement in cultural heritage activity whatsoever.

92

5. An agency and legislative framework

Non-governmental organizations (NGOs)

Finally, there are a number of dedicated NGOs that work in this sector. The most prominent of these is the World Monuments Fund, established in 1965 and currently based in New York. Its primary objective is the preservation of built cultural heritage across the globe, and it works in partnership with governments, funders and communities through fieldwork, training and advocacy. One of its key programmes is the biennial publication of a list of the World's 100 most endangered sites, the World Monuments Watch.

The Ford Foundation is similarly based in New York but has a number of regional offices in Africa. It is an extremely well endowed foundation which outlines its core objectives as strengthening democratic values, reducing poverty and injustice, promoting international co-operation and advancing human achievement. In the context of this study, funding is available for a variety of initiatives across the cultural sector, including capacity building, education, human rights and involving indigenous peoples in their heritage. While the organization is not without its critics, it has demonstrated innovation in its approach to cultural heritage in Africa.

The Getty Centre, based in Los Angeles, has a number of relevant constituent arms, including its Conservation and Research Institutes. The Getty has been active throughout Africa, advising and conducting conservation projects including the hominid trackway at Laetoli, Tanzania; the Royal Palaces of Abomey, Benin; rock art preservation in Southern Africa and various sites in Egypt and Morocco.

One of the most important agencies is the Aga Khan Development Network, a group of interlinked development agencies. Of specific relevance is the Aga Khan Trust for Culture (AKTC), which operates across the Muslim world examining mechanisms to revitalize communities through physical, social, cultural and economic activities. Currently registered in Geneva, it was established in 1998 as a private, non-denominational, philanthropic foundation. The Trust's work is based on the principles of sustainability, participation and a shared responsibility for positive change. It specifically supports the conservation of built heritage and places that further cultural development and projects that examine the connection between the built environment and culture of past and present Islamic societies. To date the Trust has undertaken work across North Africa and in various other locations in the sub-Saharan region.

*

There is thus a plethora of organizations, groups, agencies, individuals and donors involved in the African cultural heritage arena on the international stage, as well as an even wider community of social scientists. Many of these have particular agendas or areas of specialism, but all are generally working towards improving capacity and developing sustainable programmes of cultural heritage management. The above listing is not exhaustive by any means, nor does it set out to develop critiques of the work of the varying groups. Issues remain, such as the degree to which there is interaction between these organizations and the levels of success that their projects have met. It is instead presented to allow the reader to appreciate the scope of institutions involved in this area. The following chapter examines in greater detail aspects of these organizations' work under what is essentially the guise of international development.

6

Archaeology and international development practice

Previous chapters have examined the infrastructural and legislative context of cultural heritage agencies on a national and international scale relating to Africa. The complexity and diversity of these structures are readily apparent and reflect not only the sheer geographical scale of the region and its resources but also the multi-faceted approaches to cultural heritage management that are adopted across the continent. The core purpose of this study is to examine the relationship between international development and archaeology/cultural heritage in Africa (Fig. 9). It is apparent from the research undertaken that a number of specifically archaeological projects have occurred within this context. This chapter will briefly outline a number of these undertakings and examine their broader relevance to this study. Again, this is not a definitive list but rather a selective overview of projects and initiatives. One of the things that becomes immediately apparent is the extent to which certain countries depend on overseas funding and expertise. In many ways this is symptomatic of other development spheres where an effective industry has grown up around external interventions. There have been tangible benefits to this heritage interventionism, but it could also be argued that the sheer extent of external engagement with some regions has stymied indigenous initiative, stifled growth and led to a situation in which external agents dominate and guide research and practice. Increasingly non-African archaeologists are recognizing their responsibilities in this regard, and a more nuanced approach to practice is gradually emerging. Decades of

Fig. 9. The potential role of cultural heritage within the broader
framework of sustainable international development.

mineral exploration, urban expansion and industrial development programmes have severely damaged Africa's heritage
resource. Much of this occurred in an unregulated opportunis-
tic manner with little regard for due legislative process or
environmental concerns. Of particular concern have been inter-
nationally funded dam schemes, with many of the projects
across North and West Africa receiving only limited archaeological attention at a time when USAID and the African Development Bank had no policies for taking cognisance of
cultural heritage during development (MacEarchern 2001).

Thematic and international capacity
building programmes

An awareness of the sheer scale of issues facing the cultural heritage resource emerged late in the 1980s. As a consequence a preliminary needs assessment was conducted in 1996, involving over 25 African countries, and produced the Africa 2009 programme, formally launched in 1998, as a cooperative programme involving a range of African cultural heritage organizations, UNESCO World Heritage Centre, ICCROM, CRATerre-EAG and later CHDA. Funding partners include Sida, NORAD, and the Italian Ministry of Foreign Affairs, Ministry of Foreign Affairs of Finland, the World Heritage Fund and ICCROM. Further funds on an occasional basis come from various French embassies, the France-UNESCO Convention, national agencies and private companies. The core objective of the programme is 'increased national capacity in sub-Saharan Africa for management and conservation of immovable cultural heritage'. It recognizes a range of primary issues affecting the region, including institutional and legislative capacity, financial and technical resource availability, access and participation and aspects of governance. From the outset it envisaged four significant outputs: development of awareness of the resource, training of a national professional cadre working in conservation and management of the resource, an information exchange network, and the effective implementation of the programme. Four phases of the project were identified. During phase 1 (1996-1998) the programme needs and design were implemented. Phase 2 (1999-2001) introduced activities at both a regional and individual site level. The consolidation phase ran from 2002 to 2005 while the final phase (2006-2009) involved the implementation and transference of responsibilities to the regional authorities of the project mechanisms and outcomes. The range of events, projects and initiatives undertaken by the programme is certainly impressive, ranging from workshops, field survey and conservation projects, infrastructural development, increased site protection and awareness, and publication. The key measure of success of the programme will be its sustainability. This will only become apparent over the course of the next few years, once central coordination is withdrawn and individual agencies are in a position to effect internal change and development. It is certainly a truism that once many of these initiatives end the dynamic of the project withers away and many of the gains are quickly lost. It is hoped that this will not be the case here, but a strong argument could be made for the indefinite continuation of the central agency across sub-Saharan Africa in order to coordinate further cultural heritage development and manage a central capacity budget.

A similar, more specific, programme currently runs for museums across Africa. In 1991 the International Council of Museums (ICOM) organized a number of meetings in Togo, Benin and Ghana that examined the context, role and future for museums. A direct result of these meetings was the establishment of AFRICOM. From 1993 to 1998 this consisted of ICOM's programme for museums in Africa addressing issues such as collaboration, training, autonomy and the fight against the illicit trade in cultural material. Following the end of phase II of the programme the management of its structure and activities transferred to Africa and became the International Council of African Museums. After an initial constituent assembly held in October 1999, a constitution was agreed and its headquarters were established in Nairobi. Its vision is to 'contribute to the positive development of African societies by encouraging the role of museums as generators of culture and as agents of cultural cohesion'. Specifically, it seeks to promote museums in the context of global development, develop its associated profession, and promote cultural heritage while working towards its protection. From 2000 to 2006 funding was generated from SIDA while other organizations, including UNESCO, the Ford Foundation, the Getty and the Association Française d'Action Artistique (AFAA) provided additional funding. AFRICOM runs a central resource centre to address African museum professionals' needs, hosts a database of museums and practitioners and publishes its own newsletter.

Multilateral agencies

The World Bank

It is apparent that the World Bank's role in relation to cultural heritage falls into two categories: directly supported cultural heritage projects, and the infrastructural and development projects funded by the Bank that require environmental assessment and archaeological mitigation. A number of specific cultural heritage projects have been completed and a number are currently operational. In 1986 the World Bank produced operational policy OPN 11.03 to protect heritage assets exposed, for example, during Bank-supported construction activity, and invoked a series of guidance notes for supported projects to ensure the protection of sites and monuments (World Bank 2002: 30). The extent to which this policy was effective is debatable, with suggestions that little more than lip service was paid to the policy. Certainly there is little evidence of published or documented archaeological data that emerged during the subsequent phase of Bank activity in the African regions. Previously many of the large infrastructure and development projects funded by the Bank have paid limited heed to cultural heritage requirements (MacEarchern 2001) but this is slowly being addressed. In 1999 the Bank produced a framework for action on culture in development in an attempt to adopt a more proactive approach to cultural heritage. Specifically, the Bank had come to regard cultural heritage as having the potential to exploit these resources economically and link with employment creation and poverty reduction. The dual recognition of economic and societal value has underpinned subsequent policy in relation to cultural heritage.

In Mauritania a programme of cultural heritage protection and enhancement was financed to address the preservation of cultural assets in the country, establish an institutional heritage management framework and develop craft and tourism industries. These three strands, linked to policy development and the promotion of capacity, were perceived as positive contributors towards economic development and poverty alleviation. Results were variable, with tangible outputs including the registration of four cites (Ouadane, Chinguetti, Tichit and Ouallata) on the World Heritage List and the creation of a manuscript and sources database coupled with multimedia archiving of both tangible and intangible heritage. A series of new associations and stakeholder groups emerged from the process and a degree of capacity building and the development of textual guides took place. Greater national recognition for the requirement of heritage legislation and cohesion also emerged. However, much of the planned archaeological survey and mapping work did not take place owing to a failure to reach a consensus with internal and external archaeological groups and individuals on site protection strategies and site recording.

The Cultural Assets Rehabilitation Project ran from 2001 to 2007 as a Learning and Innovation Loan of $5million from the Bank to the government of Eritrea (World Bank 2008). The project's central goal was to integrate sections of the country's cultural assets into the economic development sphere. Four individual components to the project were outlined: conservation, museum and community participation activities at historic sites within the locale of Asmara and Qohaito; conservation and associated capacity and community development surrounding the built heritage of Asmara; the development of a national archival system; and investment in support mechanisms for intangible cultural heritage in the country. While the project was ranked as only moderately successful, a number of important results were achieved. Central to these was the emergence of a forum for discussion and the establishment of a network for future work and development in the country. The importance of cultural heritage in developing national identity and integration was seen as the primary output. A key lesson was that cultural practitioners operated in a disparate manner, and a unified institutional approach was identified as being central to the future successful implementation of cultural policy and practice.

A six-year cultural heritage project came to an end in October 2008 in Ethiopia. Four areas were addressed: resource supply for the development of conservation plans at the World Heritage Sites of Axum and Gondar; developing cultural resource management capacity at regional government level; facilitating the regeneration of traditional craft skills; and finally providing a project coordination unit for the above activities. A further project currently ongoing in Tunisia is developing sustainable heritage management programmes that will facilitate and develop cultural tourism. Specifically, the cultural heritage project aims to improve capacity and cultural policy provision. The programme will also address visitor infrastructural components of various heritage sites. This project is due to run until 2010.

The World Bank has a specific focus on the geographical region of the Middle East North Africa (MENA) (Fig. 10). In 2001 it published an action plan for cultural heritage and development across this region as part of its Orientations in Development series (World Bank 2001). In doing so the Bank specifically recognized the incredible wealth of cultural heri-

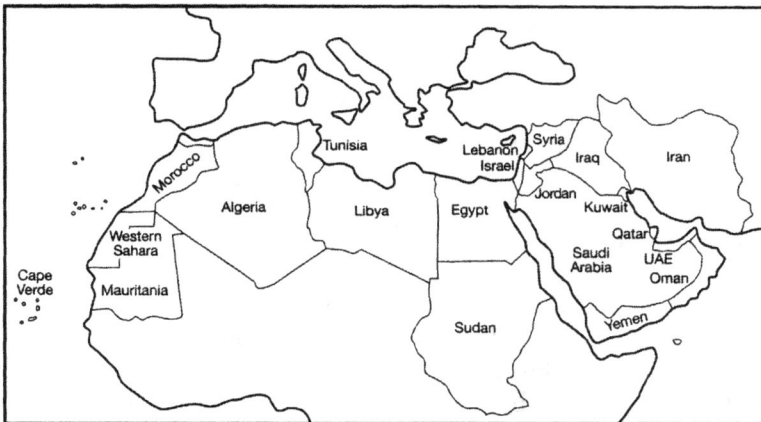

Fig. 10. The Middle East and North African (MENA) region.

tage across the region and the potential that these resources had for integration into development strategies, including urban regeneration, cultural tourism activity and heritage management. The Bank was aware that such integration would involve investment in site protection and management, capacity building and linking heritage protection and promotion with broader scale economic and social activity. Bank strategy in this regard has taken a two-pronged approach, focusing in the first instance on policy advice through the development of new policy and legal frameworks coupled with institutional and capacity development supported by partnership agreements. The second aligned approach has been the funding of cultural projects including urban improvement, cultural tourist initiatives and individual projects, all through either donor aid programmes or from private investment sources.

Country	Project	Start year	Cultural heritage component amount (US $)
Morocco	Fez Medina Rehabilitation	1998	14m
Egypt	SFD-III	1999	1m
Tunisia	Cultural Heritage and Urban Development	2001	17m

Table 6.1. World Bank MENA projects with a cultural heritage component, 1998-2007.

The Morocco rehabilitation and Tunisian heritage projects represent the main MENA projects funded over the past decade. The Fez Medina project focused on conservation and construction with the anticipated creation of thousands of jobs (World Bank 1999). While it did experience some success, the multitude of bodies involved in the work led to issues of responsibility and co-ordination, while questions also remain about the local effectiveness of the project and the expertise sources. In Tunisia a series of cultural sites were chosen for development investment. Key outcomes included the development of significant national capacity, the development of a national inventory and the integration of local community into the management and development of sites. The same issues arose across the MENA region with problems of multiple responsibility across agencies and ministries coupled with the collision of national and local area development agendas. Conservation concerns were also often subjugated to building and construction activity. Lafrenz Samuels (2009) detailed both projects in an important paper dealing with development and heritage management in the MENA region, highlighting problems with the multitude of stakeholders and development bodies, accountability, and the translative effects of these projects.

A number of external or supported agencies have been involved in the Bank's work. In 2000 the Italian government established the Italian Trust Fund for Culture and Sustainable Development (ITFCSD) to aid the Bank in its cultural heritage initiatives and facilitate the implementation of Bank policy OP 4.11-Physical Cultural Resources, which deals with Bank activities associated with heritage resources linked with Bank-financed projects. It works throughout the developing world and has participated in a number of key African projects, including the Bank's Historic Centres Revitalization Program (MEKNES), helping the Moroccan government to promote cultural tourism and regenerate historic centres with the aim of aiding poverty alleviation and improving the quality of life of the residents in these areas. Relationship difficulties with local politicians on the ground, however, resulted in IFTCSD's contribution being dropped before successful completion. As part of the Eritrean Cultural Assets Rehabilitation Project, IFTCSD was also engaged in the training of local craftsmen and is now looking towards aiding conservation of the built urban heritage of Asmara and Massawa, both of which display considerable Italian architectural influences.

Government agencies

SIDA is probably the most active of the government agencies in funding projects that link cultural heritage with development. It has run a number of thematic programmes as well as devel-

Project partner	Project/agreement type	Period and approx. support (1000 NOK)
National Heritage Conservation Commission in Zambia	Capacity building, establishment of conservation laboratory, upgrading of documentary centre	2002-2007 7,245
Centre for Research and Conservation of Cultural Heritage/Norw. Dir. for Cultural Heritage	Restoration of Facilidades Bath, Gondar, Ethiopia	2001-2007 4,521
National Archives-first phase, Malawi	Support to activities at National Archives, Govt./National Archives, Malawi	2004-2005 380
National Archives, Ministry of Finance Malawi	Support to cultural sector, with focus on restoration of monuments	2005-2008 3,820
Eco-museum/UNESCO Zimbabwe, Univ. in Bergen (NUFU-project) Zimbabwe	Facilitate participation of fishing communities in the cultural conservation and economic development in the Ancestral Landscape of Manyikaland; archaeology; education for cultural tourism	2002-2006 4,869
Ilha and Bergen (University of Bergen), Mozambique	Ilha de Mozambique: rehabilitation of historical island community, on UNESCOs World Heritage list from 1991	2002-2007 8,200
Nat. Dir. of Cult. Heritage, Mozambique (and Univ. of Bergen and Univ. of Tromsø), Mozambique	Rock art in Mozambique; archaeological mapping, research and administration of cultural heritage sites for development purposes	2003-2005? 8,140

Department of Environmental Affairs and Tourism, South Africa	Environmental cooperation programme between South Africa and Norway on various environmental areas, including cultural heritage	2000-2006 *Total programme:* 60,000
Norwegian funds-in-Trust UNESCO Ethiopia	Conservation action plan for the Rock Hewn Churches, Laibela	*USD* 299,959
Norwegian funds-in-Trust UNESCO Lesotho	Safeguarding Lesotho's cultural heritage; protection and presentation of the Ha Barona Rock Art site	*USD* 149,182
UNESCO Global	Slave route project, in cooperation with UNESCO; protection of cultural heritage; consciousness raising in schools; research and construction of museums	1998-2001 22,000
ICCROM, UNESCO Africa	Project/support to 'Africa 2009'; activities/courses to build competence, engage the communities and enhance knowledge of the importance of cultural heritage.	1998 to date c. 2 million

Table 6.2. Recent cultural heritage projects supported by the Norwegian government and its agencies.

oping research and education networks, creating bilateral partnerships and providing opportunities for individuals and groups of students and professionals. It has demonstrated considerable vision in its breath of involvement with this area and has shown an holistic approach towards development across Africa. In an innovative move it has developed a sectoral area centred on archaeology and environment. Under this programme, the Human Responses and Contributions to Environmental Change has been developed. Substantial funding has been provided for the creation of an African archaeological network involving university and government bodies engaged on a series of research-led thematic projects. Different population groups and their responses to environmental change have been investigated across East and West Africa. Originally administered by the University of Uppsala, the programme is now managed by a number of African researchers. The programme has subsequently been extremely successful in mapping, survey, disseminating new excavation data and the production of a new generation of African PhD and masters students.

The Norwegian government, through its agencies, has been one of the most pro-active supporters of cultural heritage projects. Norway developed a number of bi-lateral agreements with South Africa as part of its environmental co-operation programme, 2002-2006. As well as projects relating to environment, waste and governance, the collaboration also covered cultural heritage. This programme extends across the region, and Table 6.2 presents a number of projects of relevance to this study that have received direct funding.

USAID's programmes tend to be less thematic and instead focus on support for individual projects and partnerships. It has invested significant funds in Egypt working through the American Research Centre in Egypt (ARCE) and various country partners including the Supreme Council of Antiquities (SCA) and the Egyptian Environmental Affairs Agency. Between 1996 and 2003 over $3million was available for the Antiquities Development Project funded under the Technical

Cooperation and Feasibility Studies scheme. Conservation and preservation work was undertaken at the Pharaonic tombs at Luxor, at the medieval fort at Quseir and at the St Anthony and St Paul monasteries near the Red Sea. Further work under the same scheme examined the impact of groundwater on sites and strategies to militate against damage. Conservation, survey and advice work took place at a number of sites including flood control at Luxor in Valley of the Kings, conservation work at Bayt ar Razzaz, monitoring of the Coptic area of Cairo and documentation at Zawiya Ibn Barquq Mosque. A series of capacity building exercises have also been supported, including museum management courses and field training for SCA staff. In Eritrea the organization has supported the development of a department of archaeology at the University of Asmara (UOA) and funded a series of scholarships and faculty secondments from the USA. Under USAID's university linkage program an archaeology professor from the University of Florida has led the UOA's programme investigating Ona sites in the vicinity of Asmara dating from the period 800 to 400 BC. One of the sites at Sembel has developed a small museum supported by the US Ambassador's Cultural Heritage Fund.

Japan also has a track record in supporting cultural heritage projects as part of its international development agenda. Through its Bank for International Cooperation (JBIC) it supplies loans with concessionary terms and conditions to developing countries to help their efforts towards the protection and promotion of the environment. One such project supported in Africa is the Grand Egyptian Museum Construction Project which has received 34,838 million yen at an interest rate of 1.5%. The project's objectives include the construction of a major museum at the Giza complex to enhance cultural heritage facilities at the site and further encourage tourism and socioeconomic development. It would also take much of the pressure off the Cairo Museum, which can no longer cater for both its curatorial responsibilities and visitor pressures. Other national supportive agencies have included Poland's aid agency supporting conservation of monuments at Meroe in the Sudan.

Country	Site	Date
Algeria	Medracen and el-Khroub Numidian Royal Mausolea, Constantine	4th-3rd centuries BC
Egypt	Aqsunqur Mosque (Blue Mosque)	14th-17th centuries AD
	Shunet el-Zebib	c. 2750 BC
	West Bank of the Nile	1540-1075 BC
	al-Darb al-Ahmar District Mosques, Cairo	medieval
	Holy Monastery of Saint Catherine, Mount Sinai	6th century AD
	Karnak Temple, Luxor (ancient Thebes)	2nd millennium BC
	Khasekhemwy at Hierakonpolis	c. 2686 BC
	Khayrbek Mosque, Cairo	Medieval
	Luxor Temple, Luxor (ancient Thebes)	2nd millennium BC
	Mortuary Temple of Amenhotep III, Luxor (ancient Thebes)	2nd millennium BC
	Sultan Qa'itbay Complex, Cairo	medieval
	Tarabay al-Sharify, Cairo	medieval
	Um al-Sultan Shaaban Mosque, Cairo	medieval
	Valley of the Kings, Luxor (ancient Thebes)	2nd millennium BC
Eritrea	Darbush Tomb	16th century AD
	Kidane-Mehret Church, Senafe	12th century AD
Ethiopia	Mohammad Ali House	c. 1900
	Mentewab-Qwesqwam Palace, Gondar	18th century AD
	Rock-hewn Coptic Churches, Lalibela	8th-14th centuries AD
Gambia	James Island, Lower Niumi District	15th-20th centuries AD
Ghana	Wa Naa's Palace	19th century AD
	Larabanga Mosque, Larabanga	15th century AD
Kenya	Thimlich Ohinga Cultural Landscape, Migori District	multi-period
Libya	Wadi Mathendous Rock Art	8000-3000 BC
Madagascar	Fianarantsoa Old City	19th century

Mali	Bandiagara Escarpment Cultural Landscape, Dogon Country	multi-period
	Djenné-Djeno Archaeological Site, Djenné	3th century BC to 15th century AD
Mauritania	Chinguetti Mosque	13th century AD
Morocco	Al-Azhar Mosque	12th century AD
	Former United States Consulate in Tangiers, Tangiers	19th century AD
	Rabbi Shlomo Ibn Danan Synagogue, Fez	17th-20th centuries AD
	Sahrij and Sbaiyin Madrassas Complex, Fez	14th century AD
	Volubilis Archaeological Site, Meknes and Moulay Idriss Zerhoun	multi-period
Niger	Giraffe Rock Art Site	prehistoric
Nigeria	Ikom Monoliths of Cross River State	before 2000 BC
Senegal	Saint-Louis Island	18th-19th centuries AD
Sierra Leone	Freetown Historic Monuments	17th century AD
Somaliland	Las Geel Rock Art	4000-3000 BC
Sudan	Suakin	10th-19th centuries AD
Tanzania	Kilwa Historic Sites	200 BC-AD 1600
Uganda	Masaka Cathedral, Kitovu Village	1927
Zimbabwe	Bumbusi National Monument	prehistoric and 18th-19th centuries AD
	Khami National Monument, Bulawayo	

Table 6.3. African sites from the WMF 100 most endangered sites list.

NGO activity

To date, with the exception of two or three major organizations, NGOs have taken little cognisance of the archaeological resource and its potential integration into international development paradigms. Three organizations are mentioned here that have developed specific expertise in this field and for whom cultural heritage plays a significant role in their day-to-day activities. While the World Monuments Fund plays only a limited role on the ground in Africa it is active in highlighting the threats to the cultural resource and the issues that develop around it. One of its most effective tools is the publication of a list of the world's most endangered sites every two years. This list carries particular weight amongst the academic community and receives considerable media coverage. Table 6.2 presents a number of sites that either currently feature on the list or have appeared previously. While it is apparent that the list deals only with sites of significant importance, its geographic and chronological spread is indicative of the extent of the threat faced by the cultural heritage resource.

The Aga Khan Foundation (AKF) has been the most active of the NGOs in developing a specific cultural heritage brief, engaging in a number of major projects in Islamic African countries. One of the main strands of its work is through its museums work. The Museum Project Unit has supported the National Museum of Mali through the construction of a conservation facility, reorganization of the collections management and development of IT facilities. In Stone Town on Zanzibar the Foundation is supporting the development of an Indian Ocean Maritime Museum focussing on the geography and diversity of peoples and communication across the region. Ecology, oceanography and human interaction with the sea will be interpreted through traditional museum displays as well interactive and education facilities. One of the focuses of the centre will be the recently conserved nineteenth-century Sultan's barge. The AKF has also been actively engaged in the development of a Museum of Historic Cairo in partnership with the Supreme Council of Antiquities of Egypt centred on Al-Azhar Park, redeveloped by the Aga Khan Trust for Culture (AKTC) over the past twenty years. The museum will focus on the medieval Islamic heritage of Cairo as well as integrating into other heritage sites in the area. Conservation and training facilities have also been established at the site. Each of these facilities has been supported to promote the study of their respective heritages and to be accessible to both local communities and tourists. The AKTC has also been engaged in restoration and urban development work as part of its Historic Cities Programme, launched in 1992. A major focus of its work has been the restoration of the Old Dispensary Building on Stone Town's waterfront and a number of smaller buildings across the historic urban core of the town. The Trust has also developed a conservation plan for the town and has been engaged in the transformation of a number of open public spaces including Forodhani Gardens and Kelele Square. The Aga Khan Development Network also enabled the conversion of the former telecommunications building into the Zanzibar Serena Inn, an upper-class hotel facility. These projects represent co-ordinated efforts between the various Aga Khan units with donor agencies, the Zanzibari government and the international community.

The Ford Foundation has been active in supporting archaeological work over the past four decades. It first opened an East African office in Nairobi in 1962 with an office being set up in Johannesburg in 1993 and has further offices in Lagos and Cairo. During the 1980s funding was supplied to the National Museum of Kenya to develop training programmes and to help preserve sites and finds of importance. One of its specific goals in promoting peace and justice has been the promotion of initiatives to 'strengthen freedom of expression and celebrate diversity in heritage and identity'. Specifically, the Foundation has been active in South Africa in supporting major cultural institutions in their work of protecting and promoting historical sites and finds in that country.

University programmes

Finally, a number of Global North universities are contributing in a constructive and engaged manner with Africa and the archaeological resource. While there is extensive activity taking place across this sector on a number of different scales, a small selection of examples is presented here to provide an indication of the range of initiatives currently underway.

Uppsala University in Sweden has already been mentioned in terms of its innovative approach to development funding partnerships and its proactive approach to the training and funding of African PhD students. Few other external universities can match its approach and scope of work. Other current projects of note include the Historical Ecologies of East African Landscapes, directed by Paul Lane at the University of York and funded by the EU under a Marie Curie Excellence Grant (www.heeal.eu). This is an exemplary multidisciplinary project examining human-induced environment change over the past five millennia. It is this type of innovative project that leads to greater understanding of human interaction with landscape and provides a more nuanced understanding of past human activity, moving away from the over-traditionalist artifactually-led chronological sequencing projects that once constituted the dominant paradigm in African archaeology. A European TEMPUS-funded project establishing a centre for maritime archaeology deserves a similar mention. This innovative project identified a skills and research base need in North Africa in the field of maritime archaeology. The subsequent partnership, primarily between the universities of Alexandria in Egypt and Southampton in England, formalized a three-year project resulting in the establishment of the centre and associated teaching and research activities.

Development directions and cultural heritage linkages

This chapter will attempt to examine a number of specific themes and concerns within contemporary international development paradigms. Rather than present an exhaustive overview of these issues, we will instead look at a selection of particular ways in which archaeology and its methodologies can both contribute to these debates and offer insights into their operations and theoretical environments. Again, it is stressed that the archaeological resource will not itself change the nature of development but rather has the potential to contribute to better change within society if managed and utilized in particular ways. This in itself is contested given that certain practitioners will strongly argue against the use or manipulation of archaeology in this way and would rather let the archaeology remain as a static entity that simply requires protective curation. Such an approach has merit but the tone of this volume continually encourages moving beyond the static and engaging in a more proactive useful way with a complex and necessary resource. A number of such contributions and the work of its practitioners and the resource will be examined here in a selective promotion of future development avenues.

Heritage and value

Assignation of value to heritage is both fraught with difficulty and highly contentious (Graham, Ashworth & Turnbridge 2000). Value, of course, can mean many things and is both tangible and intangible. It is often something accepted but never questioned, with even professional archaeologists rarely questioning in depth the value of the subject and resource. There are many different ways of addressing and qualifying this value. Archaeology is an invaluable mechanism for learning about the past and has significant educational value in developing understanding of societal development and environment change. Archaeology has a community value in that an area's heritage contributes to identity and a sense of place. The built cultural resource has an intrinsic aesthetic value and can contribute towards amenity and leisure. Archaeology also has an economic value, but this aspect has rarely been addressed within academia and is difficult to quantify.

At a basic level value can be an economic entity, one that is quantified in measurable monetary terms. Alan Thomas has forwarded four perspectives on the role of the economy in the context of the international alleviation of poverty through various forms of development, outlined in Chapter 2 (Thomas 2000: 43). If one accepts development as an immanent process within capitalism then one approaches the concept from a neo-liberal perspective, laying especial emphasis on market expansion and economic development. Closely aligned to this is the role of individuals as entrepreneurs acting as the primary agents for developing profit-driven ventures, economic entities and emergent economic activity as the key to the alleviation of poverty. International development is then seen as creating 'obstacles' to the market (ibid.). The recent effective collapse of world markets has severely dented this approach and has highlighted in the strongest possible terms the dangers of a loosely regulated market dominated by a small number of elite players. In post-development thinking a rejectionist view of most forms of development and international aid exists. This school disagrees with most forms of interventionism and instead favours the natural progress of capitalism. This thinking would then naturally see capitalism and its associated economic components as being primary agents of evolving and varied development.

Here, initially, the question of monetary value and built

7. Development directions and cultural heritage linkages

heritage must be discussed. Organizations such as the World Bank will adopt an overtly economic approach to development studies and it is important to place the archaeological resource provisionally within the context of such frameworks. Lafrenz Samuels (2009: 84), for example, has strongly argued that development programmes use 'material heritage for economic growth'. There is a dichotomy here between the built heritage academic community and external practitioners. Within the community of the former there has been a general reticence to engage in discussions about the economic value of heritage. Contentious issues of commodification, ownership and responsibility are intrinsic components of this reticence, with the archaeological community largely seeing themselves in a guardianship and interpretive role rather than an exploitative and commercial one. Even when archaeologists are engaged in the commercial development process there is still a tendency to paint this activity as environmental protection and as an investigative research process rather than as a business enterprise. A certain schizophrenia has emerged, with practitioners being almost embarrassed to admit to this side of their subject. Of course in simple terms it can be seen that archaeological remains can play a significant economic role in the wellbeing of a country. At its extreme one can take the example of Egypt, where the sheer wealth of its past cultural resources is largely the *raison d'être* of its tourist industry, estimated as a $3billion enterprise (Skeates 2000: 61). In 2006-2007 tourism accounted for 27% of service industries in the country while it made up 20% in Morocco and 17% in Tunisia (World Bank 2007). Linked into this tourist activity is the capacity of the cultural resource to generate employment and create economic opportunity. While Egypt has a distinct advantage in this area given the international market recognition of its past, other countries have a similarly impressive cultural legacy, albeit far less known. Sudan has a corresponding Nile Valley historical legacy with monumentality to match that of Egypt, but access to its cultural product is severely limited by geo-political factors. The Mediterranean countries of the North African coast have been endowed with extensive classical remains matching any of the sites present along the southern French or Spanish coasts. The architectural legacy of their medieval and Islamic towns is as striking as it is accessible.

In East Africa the tourist product is dominated by the safari trip followed usually by a stay at the ocean. Here the level of cultural impact is harder to quantify. Official figures are hard to come by and even more difficult to associate with heritage. Between 1988 and 1989 804,532 visitors came to Kenya with 246,497 visiting monuments and museums (Wilson & Omar 1996). Kenyan museums during the same period reported revenues of K£477,745 with a resulting surplus after running costs of K£113,458. In 1989 24,126 Kenyan school children and groups visited monuments and museums on the coastal region of that country. By 2002 visitor numbers at other sites in other countries ranged from 120 to the World Heritage Site at Dja, Cameroon, to over 100,000 each at the sites of the Island of Gorée and Great Zimbabwe (UNESCO 2003: 49). Associated tourist benefits from these sites included hotel provision, restaurants, souvenir and craft production, guiding and curatorship.

Robin Skeates (2000) has written an important critique of the movement towards the commodification of heritage. While heritage investment can lead to job creation, spin-off industries and a raising of country or area profile, it can also be damaging. Negative impacts include alteration and damage to monuments, a diversion of resources to single sites at the expense of the broader resource (see Breen 2007), and the decontextualization or disneyfication of sites. An over-emphasis on the facilitation of tourists can also alienate local communities and lead to displacement, as seen in the Masai Mara. Placing responsibility for heritage development in the hands of developers can lead to insensitive conservation, unsustainability of management practice and a diversion of funds away from protection and research towards interpretation and profit (Fig. 11). Rachel Engmann from Stanford University suggested at WAC 6 that in West Africa such moves have led to an aliena-

Fig. 11. Interpretative signage at the German Cemetery,
Bagamoyo, Tanzania.

tion of community from heritage and the tourist industry. In countries like Ghana, castles and forts have been developed as heritage amenities but with competing narratives. African Americans come to view these sites as reminders of their slave past, while Ghanaians remember them as sites of resistance to colonialism. In recognition of the extent of trans-Atlantic visits, USAID has invested $10million at the Fort Orange site to facilitate this diasporan heritage industry that Engmann sees as effectively a neo-colonial tool.

Of course the economic value of heritage should not be measured by tourism alone. Value can also be ascribed in different contexts. 84% of World Heritage Sites in Africa convey additional heritage value to the public through community engagement, accommodating councils of elders, cultural events with film, theatre and debate, and the production of print media (UNESCO 2003: 45). The educational component of these sites is also utilized with Great Zimbabwe being visited by over 12,000 school children annually before the onset of the current instability. Six World Heritage Sites had also developed environmental education programmes by 2003, with this number rapidly growing in the intervening years.

The application of the field of environmental economics is also relevant here. This subject is normally used to produce cost/ benefit analysis of environmental industries and policies such as renewable energy and policies to deal with waste, pollution and environment change. Key to this concept is the equitable distribution of finance across society to ensure sustainability and accountability. Given the centrality of responsibility under this system, society in effect works towards the common good on an inclusive basis while recognizing the transnational nature of resources and processes such as pollution and resource exploitation. Balance and consideration is therefore required in all interaction. While this field is mostly associated with things like pollution, carbon offsetting and exploitation of common resources, the cultural resource can also be included. Built heritage is a global resource generating global interest and patronage. There is recognition of a common human ancestry and a shared past as a collective continuum. Such recognitions generate a sense of collective responsibility and a degree of guardianship. Heritage may have national or regional associations but feeds into a larger world system of human experience. The monuments of the past will never be fully understood, but they represent a product of their contemporary environment and are used and interpreted for current political needs and the assignation of formative ethnicity and identity constructs. Attempting to undertake a valuation of the resource is therefore complex and indeed contested, given the concerns of Skeates (2000) and others. A valuation can essentially be divided into two aspects, use and non-use. The sheer presence, aesthetic value and sense of place that the archaeological resource provides is immeasurable and unquantifiable, but its non-use or unavailability for exploitation gives it value to certain, if not all, sections of community. Actual usage from reorientation, visitation and curation is more tangible, and people participation can be measured through the recording of visitor numbers and the sum of fees. A particular site may generate so much in income and an arbitrary valuation can be assigned to this particular element of the resource, while at the same time recognizing its broader less tangible elements. Such analysis is increasingly being undertaken by governments, but frequently the motivation for doing so is misguided. Often inherent in this is a lack of appreciation of the resource as fragile and ever-diminishing and the irreversibility of impacts on sites and cultural landscapes. Future decision-making must then take account of future outcomes of developing the resource and the intrinsic need for management and research programmes centred on sustainable development policies. Attempting to simplify the cultural resource into a definable and manageable economic entity is probably unnecessary and misguided. Contemporary approaches should instead recognize the finite nature of the resource and its broader set of values and begin to seek mechanisms that ensure its survival while developing sustainable engagement and utilizing social capital.

Environment change

One of the most pressing concerns of contemporary society is climate and environment change. Until recently archaeologists have had a limited voice in the debates surrounding these issues, but this is changing given the recognition of both the datasets and the perspectives that they can bring to this arena (Redman et al. 2004; Rogers 2004). Of particular relevance are the temporal extent of data that the archaeological record can supply and the level of high-resolution information from specific sites and landscapes that are available. It is recognized that both landscape and society are in a continual state of change and the archaeological record is ideally placed to document this change and examine societal responses. Archaeology is also in a position to provide more recent data from the historical record with an increasing emphasis being placed on the near past within the subject.

A commonly used example of dramatic change in environment occurred in the Holocene period in the Sahara. Today the area is known globally as an extensive arid desert environment, but 6,000 years ago it consisted of extensive savannah with rivers and lakes sustaining extensive floral and faunal communities (Brooks et al. 2006). However, a significant desiccating event took place 5,000 years ago, rapidly turning the grassland to desert (Nicholson & Flohn 1980). The causes of these events are complex but are linked to a reduction in solar heating and a weakening of the monsoon linked to a change in the Earth's orbit (Claussen et al. 1999). While desiccation was rapid a number of lakes remained due to high groundwater levels and supported human activity across the region. One such site was the West Nubian Palaeolake dating from the early to mid-Holocene wet phase and formed by a substantial increase in rainfall after the movement of the tropical rainfall belt (Hoelzmann et al. 2001). This lake formerly covered an area of up to 5,330 km^2 and its margins were subject to extensive human activity between *c.* 6,300 and 3,500 ^{14}C yr BP before the lake essentially dried up. The pattern of settlement at this lake was replicated across other lesser lakes and wadis in the region. This led to an increased dependence on an ever-diminishing water resource leading to suggestions that migratory communities from the Saharan region moved north into the Nile Valley, ultimately leading to the emergence of Egyptian civilization (Hornung 1999). Such responses to significant environmental and climatic change and developing understandings of their origins are highly significant and have direct relevance to contemporary change.

While a certain amount of coastal archaeological work has been undertaken in Africa much of it has been driven by a cultural narrative agenda with little consideration of environment change. Analysis of excavation and survey projects has, however, produced a significant amount of relevant data within both published and unpublished archaeological literature. Combining these sources with those drawn from other disciplines, the data can be used to provide high-resolution analysis of conceptual models of coastal process and published sea-level curves. In particular, a number of key sea-level indicators have been uncovered during the course of excavation and survey work. This excavated evidence has clarified change over the past 2,000 years in terms of sea-level rise, geomorphological change and human response and landscape manipulation. What is most apparent is the rapid level of change over the past 200 years, associated with a combination of sea-level rise and subsidence. This information can also be used to create a substantive linkage between archaeology and international development and allow archaeologists to begin to advocate better change within policy development and societal planning across Africa. One of the best-studied areas in relation to sea-level change is the historic town of Alexandria and the greater Nile Delta. Geoarchaeological studies conducted by the Smithsonian Institution have shown that the ancient harbour at Alexandria was subject to subsidence and submergence from various processes such as eustatic movement and individual destructive events including earthquakes and storm surge through analysis of lithologic and biofacies data.

Cultural genocide

The political use and abuse of archaeology have been a theme of twentieth-century conflict. Archaeology has been used by various groupings and individuals to advance their claims to cultural superiority and ethnic dominance. Hitler and the Nazi movement, for example, used the subject to develop a pseudo image of the Aryan race as having a long and culturally dominant existence across the modern Germanic regions. The views of Gustaf Kossinna (1858-1931), advocating the definition of ethnic boundaries on the basis of material culture and the cultural uniqueness of the Germanic peoples, were widely adopted by the National Socialist Party. Such a dangerous use of the subject is not isolated and continues to emerge in a number of extreme contemporary events. Genocide was a term first coined by Raphael Lemkin in 1994, a term that derives from the Greek *genos*, meaning race or tribe, and the Latin *caedere*, to kill. The Convention on the Prevention and Punishment of the Crime of Genocide was adopted by Resolution 260 (III) A of the United Nations General Assembly on 9 December 1948. Under this convention genocide was defined as any act 'committed with intent to destroy, in whole or in part, a national, ethnical, racial or religious group'. Two further associated concepts include cultural genocide, the deliberate destruction of the cultural heritage of a people or nation for political, military, religious, ideological, ethnical, or racial reasons, and ethnocide, the destruction of a culture (including the language) of a people, rather than the people themselves. Article 7 of the United Nations Draft Declaration on the Rights of Indigenous Peoples (26 August 1994) states that indigenous peoples have the collective and individual right not to be subjected to ethnocide and cultural genocide, including prevention of and redress for:

(a) Any action that has the aim or effect of depriving them of their integrity as distinct peoples, or of their cultural values or ethnic identities;
(b) Any action that has the aim or effect of dispossessing them of their lands, territories or resources;
(c) Any form of population transfer that has the aim or effect of violating or undermining any of their rights;
(d) Any form of assimilation or integration by other cultures or ways of life imposed on them by legislative, administrative or other measures.

There is then an implicit association between archaeology and human rights given the intrinsic part the subject plays in ethnic and identity construct. Archaeology plays a central role in the formation of societies' cultural values, links them explicitly with territory and helps define their sense of place and being. Any misuse of the resource coupled with resource denigration effectively constitutes a breach of rights and collective wellbeing. Recognizing this linkage can also lead to a more proactive deployment of the subject. Gregory Stanton (1988) has identified eight stages of genocide beginning with classification, symbolization, dehumanization, organization, polarization, preparation, extermination and finally denial. While it is not proposed here that archaeology can be used to prevent genocide on its own, it can be used to inform and avoid the misconceptions and origin myths of the early stages.

The initial phase of classification involves various cultures defining society into different groups on a number of different bases including religion, ethnicity or race. Such categories can lead to bipolarization, encouraging greater division and the emergence of tension and conflict between various groups: one thinks of Catholic versus Protestant, Arab versus Jew, Hutu versus Tutsi.

Subsequent symbolization formalizes classifications through the assignation of particular symbols or labels to certain groups in society, ultimately leading to dehumanization. One recent example is the Rwandan genocide of 1994 when 800,000 predominantly Tutsi individuals were killed by Hutu militias and armed groups. This was quickly labelled both in international media and political circles as an internal ethnic conflict, yet the background was far more complex. The differentiation into two groups was largely a product of late nineteenth- and early twentieth-century colonial activity when the Belgium authorities divided society into ethnic groups, including Tutsi, viewed as cattle keeping, owning more than ten cows, and Hutu, viewed as cultivators, owning less than ten cows. This attempt to organize society was based on mythico-histories of intelligent hamite Tutsi invading Hutu lands in earlier centuries. This division was later formalized through the use of identity cards, educational programmes and employment quotas. Yet archaeology finds little evidence to support this division and shows that any division that emerged was not the result of ethnic difference but rather of the emergence of economic class distinctions. Genetics further disprove the notion of external origins while the material cultural evidence for large-scale migration or invasion is limited. In 2007 the Rwandan government's Commission for Human Rights stated that the 'colonialists took a united nation with a common culture and language and split it down the middle on the basis of a mythical racial divide. Then post-independence regimes converted this legacy into an institutionalized ideology of hatred'.

In the ongoing conflict in Darfur similar origin myths and pseudo-ethnic divisions have been used to justify war and injustice. Again both the media and diplomats have created the view that the conflict at a basal level is between Muslim and Christians, and Arabs versus Black Africans. Yet a more nuanced historical analysis of the situation reveals a somewhat different picture with the construction of arbitrary Arab ancestries among certain groups and a high degree of fluidity in terms of group labelling and identification and 'tribal' identity. Examination of the admittedly limited archaeological data from the region also shows a more socially cohesive past without any significant migratory movement of peoples. It points to the region having more in common archaeologically with the Chad Basin than the so-called Arabic areas to the east or north.

Archaeology thus has a key contribution to make to these debates. Its methodologies and findings can be used to deconstruct origin myths and break down misconceptions within divided societies. Archaeology can also illustrate commonalities as well as demonstrating the positivity of difference. Its data and physical remnants of the past can be utilized to develop educational programmes that strive to achieve understanding and cultural appreciation of difference. All too often ethnicity and identity are based on false or artificial memory exaggerated by misuse of culture and an ignorance of science. It is then a priority to conduct more informed research coupled with more nuanced dissemination of the resulting data. While the past will always remain a myth, more informed objective analysis can counter much that is dangerous in some proponents of subjective remembered histories.

Colonialism and post-colonialism

Colonialism means the control of people and territories outside one's own state, with the aim of increasing the wealth and welfare of the colonizing power (Fig. 12). The driving force behind colonialism is the extraction of resource, material or labour from the colony at a lower expenditure than would normally be attainable. In just the same way as this applies to the economic exploitation of the African continent, the extraction of the archaeological resource is also an act of colonialism, whether this is through the illegal export of cultural artefacts or through conducting research within a bubble of Northern ideology. In this way archaeology conducted in Africa by academics from the Global North has in the past been implicitly colonial. Often power relations that have appeared equal have, through the driving forward of Northern-led research agendas, spread a particularly Northern-oriented archaeology – an archaeology, as described

Fig. 12. British troops at the Sultan of Zanzibar's palace in Stonetown (*Illustrated London News*, 27 July 1880).

earlier, that concentrated largely upon human evolution and Stone Age technologies as part of an implicit colonial policy of cultural inferiorization. It is here that archaeology and historical colonialism cross, as our current understanding of colonial processes is based upon the development of Western anthropology and in just the same way as more radical and questioning archaeologies are beginning to query traditional African archaeological directions, so too have anthropologists questioned traditional colonial ethnographies and their close link to colonial powers (e.g. Barker, Hume & Inversen 1994; Benjamin 2002; Comaroff & Comaroff 1992; Dirks 1992; Gasco 2005; Mignolo 1995; Seed 1991). What these studies have in common with each other and with an important shift in current archaeology is their rejection of binary oppositions. By rejecting the traditional historical view of the 'coloniser' and the 'colonized', they have developed new ideas of socio-cultural hybridity in response to the recognition of new societies created through the colonial process. This critical re-evaluation of traditional discourses has developed into what we now refer to as Post-Colonial Theory.

Post-Colonial Theory is both a temporal and an ontological epithet and can be used as a signifier of research, events or thought that occurred post-deconstruction of the European empires in the mid to late twentieth century. It can at the same time be an academic approach whose ideology is the investigation of non-hegemonic theories of feminism, gender, ethnicity, diaspora, resistance, and non-colonialist, less Global Northern-centric views. In this way post-colonial archaeology can possess a theoretical expansiveness in the way it aims to adopt the voice of otherness included in all experiences. In doing so it can, in an African context, address a wider set of issues and appropriate data from as wide a consciousness as possible to create a multi-layered historical narrative (Fig. 13). In order to do this, archaeological practitioners in Africa must first reject traditional overriding meta-narratives and totalitarian social theories. In this way it is essential that *critical archaeological theory* be developed

Fig. 13. Detail from the Allidina Visram monument,
Mombasa, celebrating an Indian capitalist immigrant.

and researchers recognize the historically conditioned nature
of the discipline and accept and engage with the realism that
their work stands within a specific context and is generated
from a specific world-view, be it North or South. Gaining control of narratives of culture and identity is thus central to the
struggle for global equality.

In terms of its impact upon Africa, European colonialism of

the nineteenth century has left an indelible impression upon the continent's geography, politics and culture. Even a cursory glance at modern maps of Africa displays the grid-like geopolitical legacy of European partition and highlights the disregard of cultural relations when Europeans dissected the continent for economic gain. More recently during the 1960s, when many African states were driving for independence, it was the politics of the Cold War that influenced the nature of independent state governance along with a renegotiation of pre-colonial heritages. States began to adopt what Harbeson (1995) called 'syncretic self-reliance', whereby independent states attempted to incorporate the elements of Western doctrine they saw as positive with elements of their own pre-colonial identities. In this way Africa remained tied to the world-system and modernization theories of the Global North (be they East or West, communist or capitalist). This not only led to Africa's reliance on systems of Northern dominant market economics and state belief in theories of political democracy and socialism, but also formed the historical rationale for the Global North's continued engagement with post-colonial African affairs (Harbeson 1995).

One of the recurring themes of post-colonial economic reorganization in Africa was a series of 'indigenization programmes'. Idi Amin engaged in an 'economic war' against the Asian community in 1972, Mobotu Sese Seko ran campaigns of 'zairionization' and 'radicialization' in 1973-1974, Tanzania adopted a programme of 'socialization' after the Arusha Declaration in 1967, Nigeria saw a series of 'indigenization decrees' in 1972-1976, and Zaire and Zambia nationalized their copper mines during the same period (Young 1995). Whether one agrees or disagrees with the actions or processes undertaken in these post-colonial regimes, it may be considered that such actions directly focusing on resource management are an essential step in the adoption of independence. In this way, the re-negotiation of Africa's heritage resource can be viewed as a form of indigenization of a nation's material record and arguably an essential process in the movement toward global equality. However, the same criticisms of the economic policies outlined above apply to any similar application of national heritage resource management. For example, resource 'indigenization' could be said to have limited benefit for a narrow social band within the respective countries. There was also evidence in a number of instances of international disengagement and collapse (whether due to mismanagement or external political drivers), the most immediate example being present-day Zimbabwe. Finally, alienation and a lack of validity is also a threat to any regime of control and this must be taken into consideration where new archaeological narratives are being developed. The counter to this is the adoption of transparent empirical archaeological technique.

Famine

Famine studies is another area where archaeology can contribute. Not only can particular periods of famine be identified in the archaeological record, adaptive strategies and coping mechanisms by society can also be illustrated. There are then clear lessons to be learned from how past famines developed and what their consequences were. A willingness to engage in such an agenda is important for future research programmes. The stages and mechanisms with which a society succumbs to famine are complicated and diverse. Famine can be defined as widespread 'acute starvation associated with a sharp rise in mortality' (Crow 2000: 52). Until recently it has been viewed from simplistic perspectives with its cause linked to specific events like war or to environmental degradation. Increasingly current thinking views famine as a complex and multi-faceted process linked to a variety of diverse and inter-related causation factors. Amartya Sen (1981) has emerged as one of the most significant theorists in this field in recent years. He developed his understanding of the process of famine from his own personal experience of having lived through the Bengal famine of the 1950s. In particular Sen has highlighted how the concept of *endowments* and *entitlements* plays a major role in emergent famine scenarios. Endowments constitute the personal assets and abilities of an individual or family that are used to establish entitlement to food. Entitlements are the social relationships developed between differing social groups who have command over food (Fawsett et al. 2006). This can be broadly generalized as some social groups, whether defined by class, religion or ethnicity, having greater access and command over food supplies. These relationships are constructed through the processes of production, trade and exchange, or through the sale of direct labour. *Direct entitlement* then is categorized as food accessed through self-production. *Exchange entitlement* provides access to food through the sale of labour power, while *trade entitlement* comes about through the sale of produce for the purchase of food. Many sections of society during periods of crisis or change have far less secure command over food access. In particular Sen has highlighted how rural labourers were especially susceptible to the extreme effects of famine in a number of Asian events.

The key thing here is to address the factors which lead to such crises. In general there are interrelated causes linked to social, economic, political and environmental events. Ultimately we are looking at a fundamental breakdown in societal structures caused by widespread and significant disruption in both production and exchange patterns leading to a collapse in livelihoods and a significant disruption to entitlement and endowment. This process can be greatly exaggerated by war and the absence of a social representative structure. That is where a significant percentage or grouping within society lacks representation and is subjugated to an ancillary poverty-stricken existence. The resultant dominant or subjugatory social grouping will normally then lack accountability and will probably have constructed some arbitrary justificatory framework to explain their role and purpose. War in itself does not necessarily cause famine, but it can serve greatly to exaggerate upheaval. This has a particular resonance for past communities where relief organizations and advocacy were unrecognized in the hierarchical and elitist society of the time. A further issue that can contribute to the emergence of periods of famine is environmental degradation brought about through climatic change or through destruction associated with war.

Four general stages can be identified in the lead up to a famine. Initially there is a period of intense food shortage involving the complex group socio-economic, political and often environmental factors outlined above. Secondly, many sections of broader society resort to coping strategies often involving migration to obtain food and work as well as the disposition of assets and intense disruption to the production and exchange mechanisms. Thirdly, social collapse is witnessed involving mass migrations, a marked rise in mortality among the most vulnerable in society – gradually spreading to all groups – and an absence of social accountability. The final stage is more indicative of contemporary situations involving intervention strategies and may include the establishment of refugee camps and food distribution centres to accommodate displaced populations. Inevitably once entitlement hierarchies break down in the countryside and pre-existing social accountability structures collapse, people begin to migrate towards the cities where there is perceived greater availability of food supply and social stability. As a consequence peripheral settlement increases in certain areas outside the larger towns and associated shanty areas grow in size. Towns will always act as a magnet for population growth, but it is suggested here that rural displacement throughout history contributed significantly to this expansion.

Community archaeology

There has been an increased interest in the practice and development of community archaeology, sometimes called public archaeology, over the past two decades (Little 2001; Merriman 2004). It is a multi-faceted entity but essentially involves communities and groups becoming actively engaged in both the practice of archaeology leading to empowerment and opportunities for development. Community participation is about groups taking responsibility for aspects of the resource in their particular area and exploring avenues with which the resource can be utilized for the betterment of the society. This development feeds more generally into the emergent study of sustainable communities that Rypkema (2005) identifies as having a sense of community identity, a sense of evolution, a sense of place and a sense of ownership. Community archaeology does not have rigid boundaries and can be as diverse as local groups researching a particular site in an area to archaeologists utilizing a local resource for educational and even political agendas. This form of archaeology recognizes common ownership of the resource and a collective responsibility towards its protection and enhancement. Across Africa there have been a number of exciting developments in this area. In South Africa the Living Landscape project, based in the Clanwilliam area, is an educational heritage project designed to facilitate job creation and poverty alleviation centred on the local archaeological resource. The project is funded by a number of international development agencies as well as receiving monies from internal government sources. The key focus of the project is the utilization of landscape to develop learning resources about past colonialism and the apartheid regime. Spin-offs include the development of a schools curriculum, involving community in the management of the archaeological resource, and the integration of the programme into broader environmental development work. Associated job creation schemes include the creation of a rock art trail and a parallel training scheme for local guides, the establishment of a craft shop, and the use of locals as employees in the project's heritage and learning centre.

A community archaeology project was developed as an integral part of the Quseir-al-Qadim excavations in Egypt (Moser et al. 2002). Guided by the principle of involving the local people of the area in the work, a number of initiatives were developed including educational and outreach programmes, community controlled merchandising and the development of a heritage centre catering for both locals and tourists.

7. Development directions and cultural heritage linkages

Forms of participation

The appreciation of the social and economic potential of the practice of archaeology within the development sphere, as outlined in this volume, is a direct result of the growth of community archaeology, an archaeological practice that engages through dialogue and direct practical participation with geographically local peoples. In the UK it was recognized early in the development of community archaeology that individual projects should be bilateral in approach and not simply force a dictatorial research agenda upon a community. This was especially acute where the historic environment was part of a scheme of regeneration. Through the re-use of redundant historic buildings and spaces, regeneration projects can aim to improve the quality of life for local peoples in areas where recognisable economic and social decline has taken place. Such activities can, however, place too great an emphasis upon prestige sites and materials and offer greater benefit for tourists and visitors rather than directly improving the residents' sense of pride and place. It is therefore essential that the underlying ethos of community archaeology is one that allows a community's educational, social, and cultural needs to take precedence (Smardz 1997).

A seminal piece of work, on the politics of what was at the time referred to in the USA as 'citizen participation', is that of Arnstein (1969). Arnstein developed a conceptual model or 'ladder' that grades the political validity of different forms of community participation within public projects. Arnstein believed that participation by local communities in the decision-making process at the centre of local politics was a way of involving the 'have-nots' in determining how information was shared, what aims were aspired to and what programmes and resources were engaged with. All of which, the authors of this volume would argue, are central to the successful implementation of community archaeology. Arnstein proposed eight tiers of participation and non-participation, highlighting the importance of the fundamental distribution of power within successful community engagement and by extension development. They are here listed from undesirable to desirable.

133

- Manipulation; the lowest form of participation where engagement is fundamentally one way and interaction with community is based solely on benefiting the already powerful external drivers.
- Therapy; community engagement is sought in order to adjust the attitudes and values of a community in order to fulfil a hierarchical goal.
- Informing; although informing communities of options is an important step in engaging with groups, this must not be seen as the goal or final outcome as is often the case with examples such as producing pamphlets, posters and popular literature that form an 'end product' and are not designed to stimulate dialogue.
- Consultation; again, such activity is a step closer to equal participation providing participants are not simply viewed statistically and ideas generated through this process are incorporated into action plans and research agendas.
- Placation; this can take the form of the inclusion of a minority of 'worthy' communities or community members, but depends largely upon the level of inbuilt strategies within any project designed specifically to express the opinions and wishes of a community. The more open channels available to groups to outline their aims and influence decisions, the greater equality exists.
- Partnership; true partnership within a project allows for the redistribution of power through negotiation between the archaeologist and the community. In this way decision-making responsibilities are shared through the distribution of technical expertise allowing groups to make informed choices and steer research agendas.
- Delegated Power; partnership and empowerment can then lead to communities achieving the dominant decision-making role and choosing at what level they desire engagement with non-local groups. Ultimately leading to;
- Citizen Control; the final aim of all community engaged developmental archaeology. At this level the community has

both the expertise to carry out its own research and the ability to seek out and attract the necessary funds.

By deconstructing the archaeological process in this way it is possible to see how what we do as heritage researchers in Africa can be utilized as a tool of positive change. Archaeology can be a weapon in the fight against the unequal balance of powers of identity and work towards helping communities positively re-engage and benefit from their past. This kind of examination of the impact of archaeological practice also has fundamental theoretical implications for the discipline of archaeology globally. By engaging with non-traditional archaeological practices resulting from working partnerships with those from outside our immediate cultural zone (be this transregional, trans-national or trans-continental), archaeology can continue its evolutionary course in a manner that is explicitly socially oriented.

Engaged or advocacy archaeology

It has been recognized here that much archaeological practice in Africa has been guided by a Westernist and individualist agenda. However, increasingly individual archaeologists are recognizing their role and responsibilities in the development arena and are seeking out more proactive and engaged ways of engaging with society and its ills.

One of the most contentious elements of new archaeology roles in a broader geographical sense is that of archaeologists becoming involved in military campaigns. Iraq, in particular, has seen the involvement of a number of US and UK archaeologists in heritage protection, cultural awareness and capacity exercises (Emberling 2008). Accusations of people supporting the war effort through such involvement are commonplace, while labels such as 'embedded' archaeologists have also been bandied about (Stone 2008). While all archaeologists will condemn the destruction of built heritage during conflict, few are prepared to become involved in protection programmes while

135

being aligned to the military. The debates surrounding this issue are being forwarded elsewhere and are particularly promoted through American anthropological circles where the issue is highly pertinent (González 2004; 2008). The key pro argument forwarded is that archaeology as a profession is unable to stop wars but engaging with the military to train personnel in heritage protection strategies and in explaining the historical cultural context of the conflict region will enable better understandings of local culture and the need to protect the resource on the ground. The anti arguments are numerous and centre on the ethical considerations of being involved with aggressive politically driven power agendas. This is a very simplistic presentation of both sides, and readers are encouraged to engage with the burgeoning literature associated with the argument. However, simply directing readers towards such material appears like sitting on the fence so we will close this short section with a personal statement.

It is unlikely that we could ever foresee ourselves engaging with such overtly aggressive forces as the US military, but we are open to being involved in certain UN peacekeeping missions conducted by particular countries. Engaging with Irish peace-keeping forces in Chad seems very different to being involved with invasion forces in Iraq. Increasingly, most agencies involved in development and humanitarianism relating to conflict scenarios are questioning the form, approach and philosophy of differing levels of intervention. Much of this analysis is becoming increasingly difficult as the complexity of each situation is examined in an increasingly globalized and interlinked geopolitical global arena. There is little by way of consensus and both the terminology and advocated responses remain contested. Historically external agencies (excluding military forces) only intervened in conflict or disaster situations in sovereign countries by invitation or through some form of brokered agreement (Hanlon 2006b: 49). Intervention has the potential to change the outcome of a conflict and may even facilitate its continuance, a concept labelled the 'Nightingale effect'. Following international intervention in the Biafran conflict in 1968 sovereignty was breached by humanitarian agencies and by international financial institutions. In contemporary times too the very notion of sovereignty is challenged by globalization. However, following events in Nigeria forcible humanitarian intervention gave way to the concept of the responsibility to protect. This is rooted in the absolute ethical lens of interventionism.

At the base level absolutist ethics can be defined as the moral need to act. 'Deontological ethics', or absolute morality, is defined by Hanlon (2006a: 44) as the need or requirement by individuals or agencies to react to events on a morally led basis. We can further argue that it involves a moral obligation to act if those actions are viewed within the context of improving human condition, as well as promoting freedom and rationality. Of course all of these are contested notions and a high degree of subjectivity will be involved, dependent on socio-economic, personal, political and geographical factors. Nevertheless it recognizes a basic criterion of the promotion of right actions over wrong ones.

If we examine the concept of the Core Principles of Responsibility to Protect, proposed in 2001 by the International Commission on Intervention and State Sovereignty, then it does appear that interventionism be an obligation on the international community. In the case of Sierra Leone the state had failed to protect its population during a period of conflict partly caused by external international factors. The international community was most certainly very slow to react to genocide in Rwanda while the current situation in Darfur has been managed in a grossly inadequate manner by international governments and multinational agencies like the AU and the UN. In each of these scenarios it could be argued that military intervention was both justified and necessary regardless of the issues of sovereignty they raised. There was clearly a 'compelling need', forceful intervention was a top priority and *just cause* can be clearly demonstrated. The latter has been subsequently argued and effectively proven in the international courts. There is limited consensus within the 'humanitarian' community about military intervention (Barry 2002: 9). Oxfam supports such intervention only if there is no other alternative

137

to stop the widespread loss of life, such as in a genocide scenario. Médecins Sans Frontières (MSF) adopts a strongly absolutist approach, arguing that it has the capacity and responsibility to be involved only with providing humanitarian assistance and is not responsible for future peace-building activity. Somewhere archaeologists fit into this quagmire. Increasing levels of debate with the subject over the next number of years will add clarity and formalize positions.

Engaging with post-conflict heritages is also an important part of archaeology's role in developing social inclusion in Africa. As discussed earlier, this may be in the form of research into the more recent past – for example, apartheid materiality in South Africa or nineteenth-century European colonial activities in East and West Africa. One member of the South African Trust and Reconciliation Commission, Pumla Gobodo-Madikizela, put it most succinctly when he stated:

Contrary to common protestations against revisiting the past, there is an urgency to talk about the past among many of those who have suffered gross violations of human rights. Sometimes telling a story over and over again provides a way of returning to the original pain and hence a reconnection with the lost loved ones. Evoking the pain in the presence of a listening audience means taking a step backwards in order to move forwards. The question is not whether victims will tell their stories, but whether there is an appropriate forum to express their pain. (Gobodo-Madikizela 2001: 27)

Likewise, through taking ownership of the material expression of past conflicts and relationships of exploitation, African communities can engage with archaeological research and wider world heritages through independent self-created narratives. The analyses of these could contribute to the discovery of new data regarding the events of conflict and the relationships therein, as well as open channels for dialogue between previously antagonistic social and cultural groups.

7. Development directions and cultural heritage linkages

Forensic archaeology

At a less contentious level archaeologists have been involved with the forensic investigations of war graves and associated civilian burial sites. In the UK a dedicated NGO, Inforce, has been established under the directorship of Professor Margaret Cox to provide forensic anthropological and archaeological expertise for the investigation of war crime or genocide sites. One of the group's specialisms is the provision of capacity building training for post-conflict countries in forensic training. The UK charity Comic Relief has provided grant aid for one such programme in Rwanda. Inforce has also investigated graves in Kisangani, Democratic Republic of Congo. The Physicians for Human Rights (PHR) group have conducted similar work in Africa as part of its International Forensic Program (IFP).

*

We have seen that archaeology then can be much more than a dry academic subject removed from the everyday concerns of the Global South. Its resource has both tangible and intangible values that can lead to economic gain, community empowerment and the potential for development. Such usages, however, need to be carefully thought out and sympathetically implemented to ensure both the conservation and preservation of the resource. Archaeologists themselves can also work in a more engaged proactive manner, deploying their skills and research concerns in areas that can bring about better understandings of the environment and human interaction with it. Their methodologies can also be employed in the social justice arena, developing better understandings of human relationships and the investigation of contemporary wrongs. Such concerns need to be increasingly debated and acted upon when institutions and individuals are framing their research concerns.

8

Towards sustainable practice

The archaeological resource in Africa is hugely rich and diverse. The continent has been labelled the cradle of humanity, producing the evidence for our earliest ancestors many millions of years ago. Most scholars accept that modern humans emerged in Africa and spread from there across the globe. Africa is subsequently witness to the great monumental societies of the North and has seen a myriad of different societies and movements over recent millennia. Islamic and European interventions led to profound change in many parts and created an African diaspora across the world. Africa's tangible and intangible heritages bear testament to the extraordinary legacy of such activity, but it is a legacy under stress. Pressures from commercial development, neglect, treasure hunting, poor governance, external interference and a lack of resources have all led to a situation in which the continent's cultural heritage is effectively in crisis. Yet cultural heritage has an intrinsic part to play in the future of Africa and its peoples. It has a value that can be measured in fiscal terms but also in personal and more abstract ways (Fig. 14). The archaeological resource is an integral part of the African environment and its communities and needs to be both protected and managed for the benefit of current and future generations. Ultimately it is an underutilized resource that to date has not been regarded as part of broader development paradigms.

The response from the archaeological and broader heritage community to this situation must operate on a number of different scales. At a multilateral level serious questioning of existing policy must be carried out. At the core of the problem

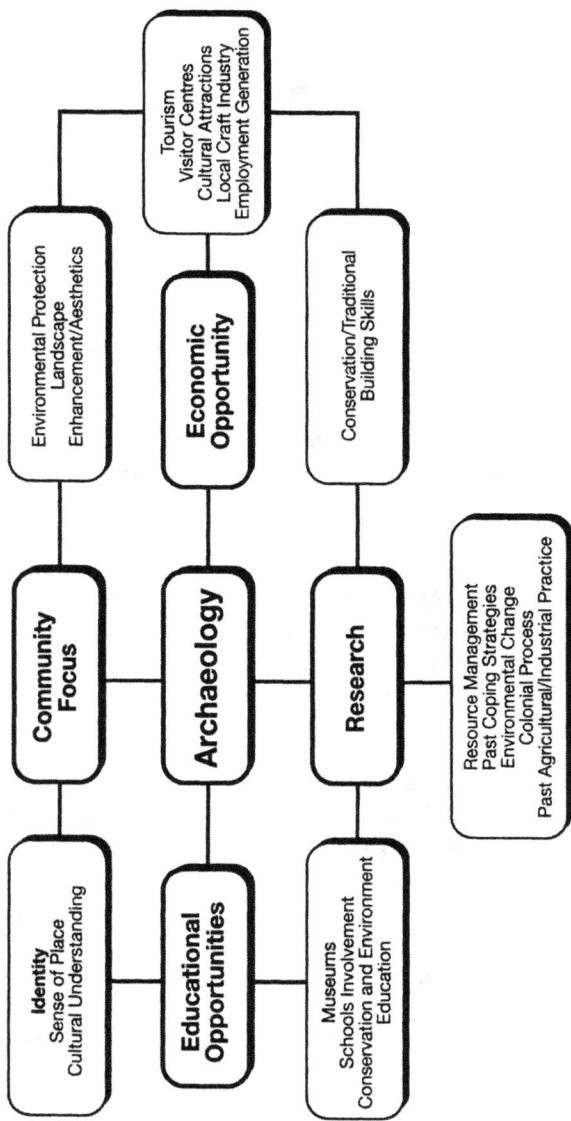

Fig. 14. The range and uses of archaeology within the development sphere.

Tourism
Visitor Centres
Cultural Attractions
Local Craft Industry
Employment Generation

Environmental Protection
Landscape
Enhancement/Aesthetics

Economic Opportunity

Conservation/Traditional
Building Skills

Community Focus

Archaeology

Research

Resource Management
Past Coping Strategies
Environmental Change
Colonial Process
Past Agricultural/Industrial Practice

Identity
Sense of Place
Cultural Understanding

Educational Opportunities

Museums
Schools Involvement
Conservation and Environment
Education

is the absence of widespread debate within the subject about the validity of archaeology in the development sphere. Elements of such a debate have emerged over the past few years (Erickson 1992; Little 2007; Sabloff 2008) but it needs to be more centralized, widespread and inclusive. The World Archaeology Congress could play a significant facilitatory role in such a debate, being genuinely international and proactively inclusive. The debate also needs to move beyond the boundaries of the subject area and involve a range of voices and practitioners. Such a debate must occur at every level within the subject, individual, institutional, national and international. Contrast this with the decades of debate and introversion within anthropology where the fundamental basics of the subject have been subject to exhaustive scrutiny (Gardner & Lewis 1996). The limited debate among archaeologists has consequently led to an absence of coherent or agreed strategies for the integration of archaeology into development practice. UNESCO plays an over-dominant role in existing practice and the unidirectional nature of its activities militates against developing broader agendas and project-driven work. For example, the Aga Khan and other foundations operate largely in isolation from the UN and rarely do the bodies come together in a co-ordinated manner. Further key issues include the lip service being paid to cultural heritage by many international organizations in the past, including the World Bank. Policies are in place within these organizations but there are rarely concrete attempts to proactively implement them. It has also been argued that the UN itself is a tool of domination, deeply rooted in the inequality of the world system, and that African state legitimacy is judged against the principles enshrined within the UN Charter (Harbeson 1995). In the same way international cultural legitimacy is too often based upon UNESCO law, an organization dominated by the Global North. The over-emphasis on and pursuit of World Heritage status is detrimental and is actively detracting from broader capacity building within individual countries (Breen 2007).

Developments in UNESCO's approach to World Heritage designations are beginning to show recognition of a failure in the labelling system. Through the Partnerships for Conservation Initiative (PACT), designed to create equal dialogue and knowledge sharing between conservation groups, the organization has been attempting to foster development in conservation based upon the UN's Millennium Development Goals (MDGs). However, as examples within this volume have demonstrated, inequality and a lack of fundamental capacity within African regions often undermine even the most straightforward of management strategies. If, therefore, UNESCO's World Heritage designation programme is to remain relevant, it must place greater emphasis upon community management, training and capacity building.

At an individual level, archaeologists must not use their research as a careerist tool simply for personal advancement. At the very least their approach to their subject matter must be more nuanced and interrogative and properly integrated into their host country's developing structural framework for the discipline; if it can also engage with community then so much the better. In this way academic funding for graduate and postgraduate research from the Global North for work carried out in the South must begin to recognize the importance of such developments as have occurred within domestic public sectors. The academic value of collaborative partnerships needs to be recognized to a greater extent, as do projects with an intrinsic social and heritage development value. Funds should also be ring-fenced for specific HER/SMR development projects as well as for the consolidation of existing endangered data.

The archaeological resource can also be considered with the MDGs. These eight goals with eighteen targets and forty indicators were the global UN led response to poverty reduction and the achievement of sustainable development between 1990 and 2015. Goals 1, 7 and 8 are of relevance here. Many of the community and public archaeology schemes outlined earlier in this volume could feed into the first goal aimed at eradicating extreme poverty and hunger. Community empowerment, job creation and resource utilization are key strategies that can be engaged. Goal 7 is geared towards environmental sustainability with key targets including the integration of the principles of sustainable development into the policies and government programmes of each country and through the reversal of the loss of environmental resources. Both preservation and conservation of the archaeological resource require due regard here. The urban conservation projects of the World Bank and organizations such as the Aga Khan Foundation also feed into target 11 listed under this goal of significantly improving the lives of 100million slum dwellers by 2020. Goal 8 aspires to the creation of global partnership for development and concerted efforts at all levels of societies to achieve and recognize common purpose and outcomes. The tone of the MDGs was further supported by the United Nations Millennium Declaration of September 2000, adopted by the General Assembly under resolution 55/2, which recognized the inequality of globalization and the need for global policies centred on tolerance, social justice and environmental sustainability.

An important resent publication by the British Academy and the Association of Commonwealth Universities (2009) entitled *The Nairobi Report* examined (through collaboration with African and UK practitioners) the state of African research into the social sciences and humanities. The report contains 22 recommendations aimed at African universities and governments, national and international funders, the UK government and universities and HE institutions. It was found that the three main areas in need of improvement included;

- Institutional foundation – poor funding for research is not the only obstacle to success, but organizational and managerial shortfalls and an institutional lack of confidence has combined with a lack of clear research agendas and postgraduate training to create a history of poor research and a lack of delivery.
- Communities and networks – collaboration and networking needs to be strengthened within Africa in order that expertise can be shared and as such must be actively promoted within research funding programmes.

- Investing in individuals – funding for research and funding for research training should not be separated and partnerships between African and UK institutions should be developed for graduate and postgraduate training which emphasize skills in proposal and grant writing as well as project management.

With these general issues of academic research in mind, a number of specific and significant heritage issues remain and require immediate attention. Resource protection is of paramount importance and requires a coordinated and agreed international response. Previous attempts at protection have been piecemeal and half-hearted at best with success levels debatable. At the core of such protection programmes lies the necessity to quantify and map the resource. While survey and inventory programmes are common across the Global North, few Global South countries have comprehensive or adequate survey programmes in place. The requirement to develop core capacity in the development of sites and monuments records and inventories of artefacts, places and landscapes is crucial. The establishment of professional staff, facilities and heritage management infrastructure is an integral part of this equation. Core capacity and resource availability at state, university and museum level is necessary.

A number of key objectives can be identified in the short term. These include the implementation of comprehensive HER/SMR schemes in each country that lacks one. Some work has been done in this arena under previous initiatives but provision remains weak and inadequate. Complimentary to this is the adoption of Environmental Impact Assessment (EIA) procedures by each country and the enforcement or enactment of EIA legislation. The absence of such mechanisms is one of the key reasons why the subject has not progressed in certain areas. Support teaching partnerships between South and North universities also need to be addressed. Existing programmes require strengthening and resourcing while provision needs to be put in place where lacking. Capacity within government institutions and museums also requires enhancement. The work of programmes such as Africa 2009 has been beneficial, but the momentum and funding behind these programmes need to be continued and improved.

Potential future developments could include the establishment of cultural units in the various state development agencies, such as DfID, Irish Aid or USAID, for example. A new international body modelled along the lines of Médecins Sans Frontières could be established to respond to international crisis where cultural heritage is severely threatened. Such a body could also play an advisory or supervisory role over major infrastructural projects across Africa where individual governments do not have the capacity or resources to oversee them. Such schemes would include dams, pipelines, road schemes or urban expansion. It is perhaps too convenient to both these developers and multilateral bodies that there is not a private heritage sector in the vast majority of countries across the continent. Some facility needs to be introduced where there is a body of archaeological expertise able to conduct this work and act as professional advocates for the inclusion of heritage components in the commercial development sphere.

Archaeology and archaeologists have the potential to engage with development. The subject and its practitioners have a key role to play in advising on landscape and resource management and investigating past and present environment change. Equally the subject's methodologies can address human responses to these changes and also have relevance for contemporary society. As archaeological practitioners and members of the global archaeological community, we have a responsibility to develop our current level of engagement with individuals and groups from outside our immediate socio-political environments and in so doing, develop the practice and theory of archaeology both for the positive evolution of the discipline and for positive social equality. Archaeology is a perfect tool by which the marginalized and excluded can be involved in challenging dominant narratives of global inequality and engage with a previously untapped material resource.

8. Towards sustainable practice

The identification of the significance and heritage value of people and places is a process that engenders shared learning and dialogue. Most importantly, it promotes *continued* learning and dialogue as individuals and communities redefine their identities throughout their lives. It is in this way that archaeology can be used to combat social exclusion and regimes of alienation.

However, the subject needs to change and begin a period of examination to address how it can play a future role in helping bringing about good change and better society. Archaeologists cannot take for granted their discipline's role and must continually strive to promote a subject that has relevance to present and future generations. Archaeologists have then a responsibility to ensure the emergence of an inclusive subject not confined to an elitist educated few in the Global North but to society as a whole, North and South.

Bibliography

Allen, N.J. (1997) 'Hinduization: the experience of the Thulung Rai', in D.N. Geller et al., *Nationalism and Ethnicity in a Hindu Kingdom: the politics of culture in contemporary Nepal* (Amsterdam: Harwood).

Allen, T. (2000) 'Taking culture seriously', in T. Allen & A. Thomas (eds), *Poverty and Development into the 21st Century*, 443-68 (Oxford: Oxford University Press).

Allen, T. & Eade, J. (2000) 'The new politics of identity', in T. Allen & A. Thomas (eds), *Poverty and Development into the 21st Century*, 485-508 (Oxford: Oxford University Press).

Allen, T. & Thomas, A. (eds) (2000) *Poverty and Development into the 21st Century* (Oxford: Oxford University Press).

Andah, B.W. (1995) 'Studying African societies in cultural context', in P.R. Schmidt & T.C. Patterson (eds), *Making Alternative Histories: the practice of archaeology and history in non-western settings*, School of American Research Advanced Seminar Series, 149-82 (Santa Fe, New Mexico).

Appadurai, A. (1999) 'Disjuncture and difference in the global cultural economy', in S. During (ed.), *The Cultural Studies Reader*, 220-30 (London: Routledge).

Arnstein, S.R. (1969) 'A ladder of citizen participation', *Journal of the American Institute of Planners*, 35: 4, 216-24.

Barham, L.S. (2008) 'Stone Age societies', in J. Middleton (ed.), *New Encyclopedia of Africa*, 102-4 (Farmington Hills, MI: Gale Group).

Barker, F., Hulme, P. & Iversen, M. (eds) (1994) *Colonial Discourse/Postcolonial Theory* (Manchester: Manchester University Press).

Barry, J. with Jefferys, A. (2002) *A Bridge Too Far: aid agencies and the military in human response*, ODI Humanitarian Practice Network Paper 37 (London: Overseas Development Institute).

Benjamin, J. (2002) *East Africa and the World: the relationship of knowledge and power in the construction of history, race and identity*, unpublished PhD Dissertation (SUNY Binghamton).

Bharadwaj, M. (2007) 'In defence of pan-Nepali identity', *Nepal Monitor*, July 22.

Brandt, S.A. & Mohamed, O.Y. (1996) 'Starting from scratch: the past, present and future management of Somalia's cultural heritage', in P.R. Schmidt & R.J. McIntosh (eds) (1996), *Plundering Africa's Past*, The Carter Lectures (London: James Currey).

Breen, C. (2007) 'Advocacy, World Heritage Sites and international development in sub-Saharan Africa', *World Archaeology* 39,3: 355-70.

Breen, C. & Lane, P. (2003) 'Archaeological approaches to East Africa's changing seascapes', *World Archaeology* 33,5: 469-92.

Bibliography

British Academy and the Association of Commonwealth Universities (2009) *The Nairobi Report: Framework for Africa-UK Research Collaboration in the Social Sciences and Humanities* (London).

Brodie, N. (2000) 'Red alert in Nigeria', *Culture Without Context* (Newsletter of the Illicit Antiquities Research Centre) 6.

Brodie, N. (2005) 'An outsider looking in: observations on the African "art" market', in N. Finneran (ed.), *Safeguarding Africa's Archaeological Past*, Cambridge Monographs in African Archaeology 65, 23-6.

Brooks, N., Clarke, J., Crisp, J., Crivellaro, F., Jousse, H., Markiewicz, E., Nichol, M., Raffin, M., Robinson, R., Wasse, A. & Winton, V. (2006) 'Funerary sites in the "Free Zone": report on the second and third seasons of fieldwork of the Western Sahara Project', *Sahara* 17, 73-94.

Caddell, M. (2005) 'Nepal – intervention in an ongoing war', in *Case Studies – TU875. War, Intervention and Development*, 60-106 (Milton Keynes: Open University).

Cardoso, F.H. (1969) *Dependency and Development in Latin America* (Los Angeles: University of California Press).

Chami, F.A. (2006) *The Unity of African Ancient History* (Dar es Salaam: E&D Ltd).

Chirikure, S. (2005) 'Cultural or physical survival? A note on the protection of archaeological heritage in contemporary Africa', in N. Finneran (ed.), *Safeguarding Africa's Archaeological Past*, Cambridge Monographs in African Archaeology 65, 7-10.

Chittick, H.N. (1974) *Kilwa: an Islamic trading city on the East African coast* (Nairobi: British Institute in Eastern Africa).

Claussen, M., Kubatzki, C., Brovkin, V., Ganopolski, A., Hoelzmann, P. & Pachur, H.J. (1999) 'Simulation of an abrupt change in Saharan vegetation in the mid-Holocene', *Geophysical Research Letters* 26, 2037-40.

Comaroff, J. & Comaroff, J. (1992) *Ethnography and the Historical Imagination* (Boulder: Westview Press).

Coombes, A.E. (2003) *History After Apartheid: visual culture and public memory in a democratic South Africa* (Johannesburg: Witwatersrand University Press).

Crow, B. (2000) 'Understanding famine and hunger', in T. Allen & A. Thomas (eds), *Poverty and Development into the 21st Century*, 51-74 (Oxford: Oxford University Press).

DeCorse, C.R. (ed.) (2001) *West Africa during the Atlantic Slave Trade* (London: Leicester University Press).

DfID (2001) *The Causes of Conflict in Sub-Saharan Africa* (London).

DfID (2006) *Country Profile – Nepal*, accessed July 2007: http://www.dfid.gov.uk/countries/asia/nepal.asp

Dirks, N.B. (ed.) (1992) *Colonialism and Culture* (Michigan: University of Michigan Press).

During, S. (ed.) (1999) *The Cultural Studies Reader* (London: Routledge).

Emberling, G. (2008) 'Archaeologists and the military in Iraq, 2003-2008: compromise or contribution', *Archaeologies* 4, 3: 445-60.

Erickson, C.L. (1992) 'Applied archaeology and rural development: archae-

Bibliography

ology's potential contribution to the future', *Journal of the Steward Anthropological Society* 20: 1-12.

Escobar, A. (1995) *Encountering Development: the making and unmaking of the Third World* (Princeton: Princeton University Press).

Fawsett, S., Kelly, B. & Wilson, G. (2006) *Development: context and practice – study guide* (Milton Keynes: Open University).

Feierman, S. (2002) *The Shambaa Kingdom, A History* (Dar es Salaam).

Finneran, N. (2005) 'Problems and possibilities in the protection of archaeological landscapes: the Ethiopian experience in a wider context', in N. Finneran (ed.), *Safeguarding Africa's Archaeological Past*, Cambridge Monographs in African Archaeology 65, 11-16.

Gardner, K. & Lewis, D. (1996) *Anthropology, Development and the Postmodern Challenge* (London: Pluto Press).

Garlake, P. (1982) *Great Zimbabwe* (Harare: Zimbabwe Publishing House).

Gasco, J.L. (2005) 'Spanish colonialism and processes of social change in Mesoamerica', in G.J. Stein (ed.), *The Archaeology of Colonial Encounters, Comparative Perspectives*, 69-108 (Oxford: Oxford University Press).

Gasper, D. (2004) *The Ethics of Development: from economism to human development* (Edinburgh: Edinburgh University Press).

Gelb, L.H. & Rosenthal, J.A. (2003) 'The rise of ethics in foreign policy', *Foreign Affairs* 82:3, 2-7.

Gellner, D.N. (2005) 'Ethnic rights and politics in Nepal', *Himalayan Journal of Sociology and Anthropology* 2: 1-17.

Gellner, D.N. (2007) 'Nepal and Bhutan in 2006: a year of revolution', *Asian Survey* 47,1: 80-6.

Gilbert, E. (2004) *Dhows and the Colonial Economy of Zanzibar* (Oxford: James Currey).

Gobodo-Madikizela, P. (2001) 'Traumatic memory', in J. Edelstein (ed.), *Trust and Lies: stories from the Truth and Reconciliation Commission in South Africa* (New York: New Press).

González, R. (2008) 'Opposing "World War III" ', *Anthropology News* 49, 2: 4-5.

González, R. (ed.) (2004) *Anthropologists in the Public Sphere: speaking out on war, peace and American power* (Austin: University of Texas Press).

Gore, C. (2005) 'A question of value: Nigerian museums', in N. Finneran (ed.), *Safeguarding Africa's Archaeological Past*, Cambridge Monographs in African Archaeology 65, 17-24.

Gosden, C. (2001) 'Postcolonial archaeology: issues of culture, identity and knowledge', in I. Hodder (ed.), *Archaeological Theory Today*, 241-61 (Cambridge: Polity Press).

Gowlett, J.A.J. (2008) 'Tools and technologies', in J. Middleton (ed.), *New Encyclopedia of Africa*, 98-102 (Farmington Hills, MI: Gale Group).

Graham, B., Ashworth, G.J., Turnbridge, J.E. (2000) *A Geography of Heritage: power, culture and economy* (London: Arnold).

Bibliography

Gundu, Z.A. (2008) 'Archaeology in the Nigerian university: international lessons and emerging curriculum issues', *African Diaspora Archaeology Network September Newsletter*, 1-12.

Gurr, T.R. (2000) 'Ethnic warfare on the wane', *Foreign Affairs* 79:3, May/June.

Hachhethu, K. (nd) 'Nepal: confronting Hindu identity', *South Asian Journal*.

Hain, P. (2002) 'Embrace global action', *The Guardian*, 9 February.

Hall, M. (1988) 'Archaeology under apartheid', *Archaeology* 41, 62-4.

Hall, M. (1993) 'The archaeology of colonial settlement in Southern Africa', *Annual Review of Anthropology* 22, 177-200.

Hall, M. (2001a) 'Cape Town's District Six and the archaeology of memory', in R. Layton, P. Stone & J. Thomas (eds), *The Destruction and Conservation of Cultural Property*, 298-311 (London: Routledge).

Hall, M. (2001b) 'Social archaeology and the theatres of memory', *Journal of Social Archaeology* 1, 50-61.

Hall, M. (2006) 'Identity, memory and countermemory: the archaeology of an urban landscape', *Journal of Material Culture* 11, 1:2, 189-209.

Hall, S. (1990) 'Cultural identity and diaspora', in J. Rutherford (ed.), *Identity, Community, Culture, Difference*, 222-37 (London: Lawrence & Wishart).

Hall, S. (1995) 'New cultures for old', in D. Massey & P. Jess (eds), *A Place in the World? Places, Cultures and Globalization*, 175-214 (Oxford: Oxford University Press).

Hall, S. (1996) 'Introduction: Who needs "identity"?', in S. Hall & P. du Gay (eds), *Questions of Cultural Identity*, 1-7 (London: Sage Publications).

Hanlon, J. (2006a) '200 wars and the humanitarian response', in H. Yanacopulos & J. Hanlon (eds), *Civil War, Civil Peace*, 18-48 (Milton Keynes: James Currey).

Hanlon, J. (2006b) 'Intervention', in H. Yanacopulos & J. Hanlon (eds), *Civil War, Civil Peace*, 49-71 (Milton Keynes: James Currey).

Hanlon, J. (2006c) 'Ethncity and identity', in H. Yanacopulos & J. Hanlon (eds) *Civil War, Civil Peace*, 95-109 (Oxford, James Currey).

Harbeson, J.W. (1995) 'Africa in world politics: amid renewal, deepening crisis', in J.W. Harbeson & D. Rothchild (eds), *Africa in World Politics: post-Cold War challenges*, 3-22 (Boulder: Westview Press).

Henry, L. (2006) 'Critical reviews of poverty and development into the 21st century', 117-20, in *TU871. Development: context and practice* (Milton Keynes: Open University).

Hodder, I. (ed.) (2001) *Archaeological Theory Today* (Cambridge: Polity Press).

Hoelzmann P., Keding, B., Berke, H., Kropelin, S. & Kruse, H.J. (2001) 'Environmental change and archaeology: lake evolution and human occupation in the Eastern Sahara during the Holocene', *Palaeogeography, Palaeoclimatology, Palaeoecology* 169: 3, 193-217(25).

Holl, A.F.C. (1995) 'African history: past, present and future', in P.R. Schmidt & T.C. Patterson (eds), *Making Alternative Histories: the prac-*

Bibliography

tice of archaeology and history in non-western settings, School of American Research Advanced Seminar Series, 183-212 (Santa Fe, New Mexico).

Hornung, E. (1999) *History of Ancient Egypt* (Edinburgh: Edinburgh University Press).

Horton, M. (2008) 'Archaeology', in J. Middleton (ed.), *New Encyclopedia of Africa,* 91-8 (Farmington Hills, MI: Gale Group).

Hughes, L. (2007) 'A brief overview of heritage in Kenya and Africa', 'Heritage, Museums and Memorialisation in Kenya, Exploring the past in the present', Museums and Heritage Research Workshop, 20-21 July 2007, USIU electronic document, accessed December 2008: http://www.open.ac.uk/Arts/fergusoncentre/memorialisation/nairobi07/index.html.

ICOMOS (2007) *Climate Change Initiatives: A Cooperative Project with International Committees, Heritage at Risk* (Paris).

ICRC (2005) Digital document, accessed July 2007: http://www.icrc.org/ihl.nsf/COM/375-590006?OpenDocument

Insoll, T. (1996) *Islam, Archaeology and History, Gao Region (Mali) AD 900-1250,* BAR International Series 647 (Oxford).

IPCC (2001) *The Regional Impacts of Climate Change: an assessment of vulnerability* (The Hague).

Joffroy, T. and Moriset, S. (1995) *Palais royaux d'Abomey 1. Circonstances et processus de dégradation (Prema-Abomey)* (Paris: ICCROM/CRATerre-EAG/UNESCO).

Joffroy, T. and Moriset, S. 1996. *Palais royaux d'Abomey 2. Guide d'entretien (projet Prema-Bénin II)* (Paris: ICCROM/CRATerre-EAG/UNESCO).

Klausmeier, A., Purbrick, L. and Schofield, J. (2006) 'Reflexivity and record: re-mapping conflict archaeology', in A. Klausmeier, L. Purbrick & J. Schofield (eds), *Re-Mapping the Field: new approaches in conflict archaeology* (Berlin: Westkreuz-Verlag).

Knudson, R. (1999) 'Cultural Resource Management in context', *Archives and Museum Informatic* 13:3-4, 359-81.

Kusimba, C.M. (1999) *The Rise and Fall of Swahili States* (London: AltaMira).

Lafrenz Samuels, K. (2009) 'Trajectories of development: international heritage management of archaeology in the Middle East and North Africa', *Archaeologies* 5:1, 68-91.

LaGamma, R. (1996) 'Africa's vanishing cultural heritage', in P.R. Schmidt & R.J. McIntosh (eds) *Plundering Africa's Past,* The Carter Lectures, 94-8 (London: James Currey).

Larocca, A. (2005) 'Conservation of rock art in the Sahara', in N. Finneran (ed.) *Safeguarding Africa's Archaeological Past,* Cambridge Monographs in African Archaeology 65, 27-32.

La Riche, W. (1997) *Alexandria: The Sunken City* (London: Weidenfeld & Nicolson).

Lane, P. (2008) 'Historical archaeology', in J. Middleton (ed.), *New Encyclopedia of Africa,* 10406 (Farmington Hills, MI: Gale Group).

Bibliography

Little, B.J. (2007) *Historical Archaeology: Why the Past Matters* (Walnut Creek, CA: Left Coast Press).

Little, B.J. (ed.) (2001) *Public Benefits of Archaeology* (Gainesville: University Press of Florida).

MacDonald, K. (2005) 'A personal perspective on ethics and the African archaeologist', in N. Finneran (ed.), *Safeguarding Africa's Archaeological Past*, Cambridge Monographs in African Archaeology 65, 33-6.

MacEarchern, S. (2001) 'Cultural resource management and Africanist archaeology', *Antiquity* 75, 289: 866-71.

McGrew, A. (2000) 'Sustainable globalization? The global politics of development and exclusion in the New World Order', in T. Allen & A. Thomas, *Poverty and Development into the 21st Century*, 345-64 (Oxford: Oxford University Press).

McIntosh, R.J. (1996) 'Excising the rot of cultural genocide', in P.R. Schmidt & R.J. McIntosh (eds), *Plundering Africa's Past*, The Carter Lectures, 45-63 (London: James Currey).

McIntosh, S.K. (1993) 'Archaeological heritage management and site inventory systems in Africa', *Journal of Field Archaeology* 20: 500-4.

McIntosh, S.K. (1992) 'Archaeological heritage management and site inventory systems in Africa: the role of development', in I. Seragelden & J. Taboroff (eds), *Culture and Development in Africa* 2: 391-414 (Washington DC: World Bank).

Malan, A. & Klose, J. (2003) 'Nineteenth century ceramics in Cape Town, South Africa', in S. Lawrence (ed.), *Archaeologies of the British: explorations of identity in Great Britain and its colonies, 1600-1945*, 191-210 (London: Routledge).

Merriman, N. (ed.) (2004) *Public Archaeology* (London: Routledge).

Meskell, L. (2001) 'Archaeologies of identity', in I. Hodder (ed.), *Archaeological Theory Today*, 187-213 (Cambridge: Polity Press).

Mignolo, W.D. (1995) *The Darker Side of the Renaissance: literacy, territoriality, and colonization* (Michigan: University of Michigan Press).

Mitchell, P. (2005) 'Managing on scarce resources: the past record, present situation and future prospects of archaeological resource management in Lesotho', in N. Finneran (ed.), *Safeguarding Africa's Archaeological Past*, Cambridge Monographs in African Archaeology 65, 37-46.

Moser, S., Glazier, D., Phillips, J.E., el Nemr, L.N., Mousa, M.S., Rascha, N.A., Richardson, S., Conner, A. & Seymour, M. (2002) 'Transforming archaeology through practice: strategies for collaborative archaeology and the Community Archaeology Project at Quseir, Egypt', *World Archaeology*, 34, 2: 220-48.

Nadeau, B. (2006) 'The curse of approval', *Newsweek International*, 10-17 April.

Nicholson, S.E. and Flohn, H. (1980) 'African environmental and climatic changes and the general atmospheric circulation in Late Pleistocene and Holocene', *Climatic Change* 2, 313-48.

Palmer, T.G. (2004) *Globalisation and Culture: homogeneity, diversity,*

Bibliography

identity, liberty, The Liberal Institute of the Friedrich Naumann Foundation, Occasional Paper 2 (Potsdam).

Phillipson, D.W. (2005) *African Archaeology* (Cambridge: Cambridge University Press).

Posnansky, M. (1996) 'Coping with the collapse in the 1990s', in P.R. Schmidt & R.J. McIntosh (eds), *Plundering Africa's Past*, The Carter Lectures, 143-63 (London: James Currey).

Potter, R.B., Binns, T., Elliott, J.A. & Smith, D. (2008) (3rd edn) *Geographies of Development* (Harlow: Pearson Education).

Pwiti, G. (1996) *Continuity and Change: an archaeological study of farming communities in northern Zimbabwe AD 500-1700*, Studies in African Archaeology 13, Doctoral thesis, Department of Archaeology (Uppsala University).

Redman, C.L. et al. (eds) (2004) *The Archaeology of Global Change: the impact of humans on their environment* (Washington DC: Smithsonian Books).

Rogers, D.J. (2004) 'The global environmental crisis: an archaeological agenda for the 21st century', in C.L. Redman et al. (eds), *The Archaeology of Global Change: the impact of humans on their environment*, 271-7 (Washington DC: Smithsonian Books).

Rugumamu, S.M. (2005) *Globalization Demystified: Africa's possible development future* (Dar es Salaam: Dar es Salaam University Press).

Rypkema, D. (2005) *Cultural Heritage and Sustainable Economic and Social Development*, accessed 2008: http://www.europanostra. org/downloads/speeches/donovan-rypkema_keynote_address_07dec_0 5.pdf

Sabloff, J.A. (2008) *Archaeology Matters: action archaeology in the modern world* (Walnut Creek, CA.: Left Coast Press).

SARIMA (2009) www.sarima.co.za: website of the South African Research and Innovation Management Association (SARIMA), accessed 2009.

Schimdt, P.R. (1995) 'Using archaeology to remake history in Africa', in P.R. Schmidt & T.C. Patterson (eds) *Making Alternative Histories: the practice of archaeology and history in non-western settings*, School of American Research Advanced Seminar Series 119-48 (Santa Fe, New Mexico).

Schimdt, P.R. (1996) 'The human right to a cultural heritage', in P.R. Schmidt & R.J. McIntosh (eds), *Plundering Africa's Past*, The Carter Lectures, 18-28 (London: James Currey).

Schmidt, P.R. & McIntosh, R.J. (eds) (1996) *Plundering Africa's Past*, The Carter Lectures (London: James Currey).

Schmidt, P.R. & Patterson, T.C. (eds) (1995) *Making Alternative Histories: the practice of archaeology and history in non-western settings*, School of American Research Advanced Seminar Series (Santa Fe, New Mexico).

Seed, P. (1991) 'Colonial and postcolonial discourse', *Latin American Research Review* 26, 3: 181-200.

Sen, A. (1981) *Poverty and Famines: an essay on entitlement and deprivation* (Oxford: Oxford University Press).

Bibliography

Shackley, M. (2001) 'Potential futures for Robben Island: shrine, museum or theme park', *International Journal of Heritage Studies* 7:4, 355-63.

Shepherd, N. (2002) 'The politics of archaeology in Africa', *Annual Review of Anthropology* 31, 189-209.

Sherriff, A. (1987) *Slaves, Spices and Ivory in Zanzibar* (London: James Currey).

Sherriff, A. (ed.) (1995) *The History and Conservation of Zanzibar Stone Town* (London: James Currey).

Shepherd, N. (2007) 'Archaeology dreaming', *Journal of Social Archaeology* 7: 1, 3-28.

Shyllon, F. (1996) 'Cultural heritage legislation and management in Nigeria', *International Journal of Cultural Property* 5, 235-68.

Sidi, A.O. (2006) 'Timbuktu: mosques face climate challenges', *World Heritage Review* 42: 12-17.

Sidibé, S. (1996) 'The fight against the plundering of Malian cultural heritage and illicit exploration', in P.R. Schmidt & R.J. McIntosh (eds), *Plundering Africa's Past*, The Carter Lectures, 79-86 (London: James Currey).

Skeates, R. (2000) *Debating the Archaeological Heritage* (London: Duckworth).

Smardz, K.E. (1997) 'The past through tomorrow: interpreting Toronto's heritage to a multicultural public', in J.H. Jameson Jnr (ed.), *Presenting Archaeology to the Public: digging for truths* (California: AltaMira Press).

Smith, L. (2004) *Archaeological Theory and the Politics of Cultural Heritage* (London: Routledge).

Stahl, A.B. (2009) 'The slave trade as practice and memory. What are the issues for archaeologists?, in C.M. Cameron (ed.), *Invisible Citizens: captives and their consequences* (Salt Lake City: University of Utah Press).

Stanton, G. (1988) 'The eight stages of genocide', *Yale Genocide Studies Series*, GS01, February.

Stockton, N. (1998) 'In defence of humanitarianism', *Disasters* 22, 4: 352-60.

Stone, P. (2008) 'Heritage protection: have we learnt the lessons of Iraq', *British Archaeology* 103: 44-50.

Tassie, G. (2005) 'Egyptian cultural heritage: let's work together', in N. Finneran (ed.), *Safeguarding Africa's Archaeological Past*, Cambridge Monographs in African Archaeology 65, 47-54.

Thomas, A. (2000) 'Meanings and views of development', in T. Allen & A. Thomas (eds), *Poverty and Development into the 21st Century*, 23-50 (Oxford: Oxford University Press).

Thomas, A. (2001) 'NGOs and their influence on environmental policies in Africa', in A. Thomas et al., *Environmental Policies and NGO Influence*, 1-22.

Thomas, G. (2007) 'A new Nepal', *Developments* 38: 9.

UNESCO (2002) *Johannesburg Declaration on World Heritage in Africa and Sustainable Development* (Paris: UNESCO).

Bibliography

UNESCO (2003) *Periodic Report, Africa World Heritage Reports 3* (Paris: UNESCO).

UNESCO (2006a) *World Heritage Report, news*, electronic document, accessed December 2006: http://whc.unesco.org/en/news/253-

UNESCO (2006b) *World Heritage in Danger*, electronic document, accessed December 2006: http://whc.unesco.org/en/danger/-

Wallerstein, I. (1974) *The Modern World-System I* (New York: Academic Press).

Wallerstein, I. (1980) *The Modern World-System II* (New York: Academic Press).

Wallerstein, I. (1989) *The Modern World-System III: the second era of great expansion of the capitalist world economy, 1730-1840s* (London: Academic Press).

WARIMA (2009) www.warima.org: website of the West of Africa Research and Innovation Management Association, accessed 08/05/09.

Wilson, T.H. & Omar, A.L. (1996) 'Preservation of cultural heritage on the East African coast', in P.R. Schmidt & R.J. McIntosh (eds), *Plundering Africa's Past*, The Carter Lectures, 225-49 (London: James Currey).

World Bank (1999) *Morocco Fés-Medina Rehabilitation Project*, Project Appraisal Document (Washington DC).

World Bank (2001) *Cultural Heritage and Development: a framework for action in the Middle East and North Africa*, The International Bank for Reconstruction and Development (Washington DC).

World Bank (2002) *World Bank Annual Report* (Washington DC).

World Bank (2006) *Physical Cultural Resources*, Operational Manual OP 4.11 (Washington DC).

World Bank (2007) *Middle East and North Africa: economic developments and prospects* (Washington DC).

World Bank (2008) *Implementation Completion and Results Report on a Learning and Innovation Loan to the State of Eritrea for a Cultural Assets Rehabilitation Project*, Report no. IDA-35470 (New York).

World Heritage Committee (2006) *Predicting and Managing the Effects of Climate Change on World Heritage* (Paris: UNESCO).

Worth, A. (2008) 'Industrial archaeology', in J. Middleton (ed.), *New Encyclopedia of Africa*, 108-9 (Farmington Hills, MI: Gale Group) .

Yanacopulos, H. & Hanlon, J. (2006) *Civil War, Civil Peace* (Milton Keynes: James Currey).

Young, C. (1995) 'The heritage of colonialism', in J.W. Harbeson & D. Rothchild (eds), *Africa in World Politics: post-Cold War challenges*, 23-40 (Boulder: Westview Press).

Index

This index contains the countries and principal site names, organizations and researchers mentioned in the text.

Index

www.ingramcontent.com/pod-product-compliance
Lightning Source LLC
Chambersburg PA
CBHW062037270326
41929CB00014B/2458